Handbook of Individual Family Constellations

MARCO MORETTI

DANIELA POGGIOLI

Copyright © 2017 Marco Moretti & Daniela Poggioli.
Translation from italian by Vivien Reid Ferrucci.
Original title: Manuale di Costellazioni Familiari Individuali,
Alpes Italia, Roma, 2015.
All Hellinger's quotes have been retranslated.
Cover photo by © Luigi Bussolati, 2017.

ALL RIGHTS RESERVED

ISBN-13: 978-1546964421

*"To see a world in a grain of sand
and a heaven in a wild flower,
hold infinity in the palm of your hand,
and eternity in an hour".*

William Blake

Contents

Preface by Jutta ten Herkel — VII
Introduction by Marco Moretti and Daniela Poggioli — IX

PART ONE – Theory

Bert Hellinger's Family Constellations (Marco Moretti) — 3
   Sources and techniques — 4
The Knowing Field (Marco Moretti) — 19
   Planes of Consciousness — 27
Orders of Love and of Helping (Moretti – Poggioli) — 43
   Right to belong — 45
   Hierarchical structure — 51
   Balance between give and take — 57
   Orders of Helping — 62
Individual Systemic Interview (Moretti – Poggioli) — 83
Wisdom (Bert Hellinger) — 103

PART TWO – Practice

Individual Family Constellations (Moretti – Poggioli) — 107
   When, which, how and why to use one of these techniques — 112
   Limitations and advantages of the Individual Family Constellations — 124
The Silent Helpers: Use of the Dolls (Daniela Poggioli) — 127
   How I proceed — 133
   Marco and Alice — 138
   Gianni: son or husband? — 141
   Sara: I want my consistency — 143
Use of Sheets of Paper (Marco Moretti) — 149
   How I proceed — 149
   Giovanna and her son's headaches — 158
Free Space (Marco Moretti) — 165
   How I proceed — 166
   Virginia the quick-tempered — 169

Visualization (Marco Moretti) 177
    How I proceed 180
    Healing the Inner Family 181
    Inner Constellation 187
    Ascent and Dialogue with the Self 192
    Brigitta and the family inheritance 195

Conclusions 199

References 201

Preface

Having read this book I feel that both, Marco Moretti and Daniela Poggioli have brought together their many years of therapeutic skill and experience. They have provided a very inspiring first manual of systemic thinking and practice in Individual settings.

Their readers will be guided sensitively and skillfully on a journey of self-discovery and new ways of looking at their own family systems.

The authors have covered the most important aspects of Systemic Constellations very well, including:

The philosophy – an understanding of the role of belonging, the power of loyalty, the principles that apply to relationships and the effect of entanglements and trauma over generations.

The practice – the relevance of spatial relationships, the field, the phenomenon of representative experience, and any symbolic representation or visualization.

With this book the authors are opening doors for those who are looking for new insights in their personal life and their relationships. At the same time they are offering practitioners a valuable manual for systemic work in individual settings.

The challenge for a facilitator is not to interpret but to explore, not to go faster than the client can participate and has energy for, to find ways of deepening the observations via sentences, to notice the way the client is absorbing and responding at a bodily level. In reading Moretti's and Poggioli's case histories I felt that they elegantly negotiated these challenges.

Both authors are inviting the reader to follow the journeys of self-discovery, insight and at the same time are giving encouragement towards a next step on a path of healing; using amongst other tools a systemic lens based on their knowledge and experience of the underlying principles of this work.

I enjoyed following their step by step processes and the description of their client work.

With all my best wishes that this little gem may find its way into many hands and hearts.

Jutta ten Herkel,
February 2015

Introduction

This book is an answer to a demand: for a teaching manual in the use of the Family Constellations method in individual treatment.

One day a colleague of mine (Marco), interested in Family Constellations, asked me for supervision of a case using an Individual Constellation. I guided her in the exploration and understanding of her client's experience and in identifying the systemic origin of an important problem the client had. At the end of this work she was enthusiastic, and she asked me if a manual for learning all the techniques of Individual Family Constellations existed. After a moment's reflection I said that none had so far been published in Italian. So I said to myself: "Well, I could write one".

I considered how this book might come into being and realized I needed collaboration. Daniela came to mind straightaway, because she is an expert in Individual Constellations with the use of dolls, and she has training in the systemic-relational approach. And like me, she has been following Bert Hellinger since his earliest educational workshops in Italy.

My approach is biosystemic and psychosynthetic, and for many years I have organized workshops in group Family Constellations. I also make much use of Individual Constellations with sheets of paper, space, and visualization.

Daniela's contribution would make this book more complete. And right away I sent her a text message, asking her if she was interested in writing this book with me.

I (Daniela) had recently finished a ten-year stint organizing workshops in Constellations at my studio, and was a little disoriented, when Marco's message arrived. I read it several times; it was true: Marco was proposing that I write a book on Family Constellations.

My first reaction was a warm-hearted smile.

The second: panic.

The third: "Why not? I have worked a lot these last 14 years and can at last share my experience with others."

It is May 2000, in the Aula Magna of Verona University, and hundreds of people are seated in a semicircle, participating in a Family Constellations workshop led by a German man, Bert Hellinger. I am totally in the dark about what is to happen and have no idea what to expect.

14 years have passed and I have not stopped attending workshops and courses in Constellations, mainly to learn how to integrate this new method into my clinical work as an individual systemic-relational therapist.

Thanks to the work of many therapists, counselors, educators, and other professionals, the Constellations have evolved, and have enriched and influenced other methods and models in therapeutic relations.

Introduction

The time is now ripe for applying the Constellations method to the individual field as well. We shall give ample testimony to this in the text.

This book has been a chance to reconsider and reorganize years of work, and especially to share with "experts", in a simple, clear and essential way, the various techniques of Individual Family Constellations. For this reason we present many clinical examples, and explain concretely how to put these techniques into practice. The result is an integrated systemic method for use in individual work.

In Part One we describe the theoretical aspects of Family Constellations: the sources, the Knowing Field, the Orders of Love and of Helping, and the characteristics of the individual systemic session. In Part Two we explain what the Individual Constellations are; when, why and how to apply them; and we describe the main techniques that use dolls, sheets of paper, free space, and visualization.

It is wonderful to show our own achievements. To have others share in our joy. If others are happy too, we are all the happier. [...] We feel inwardly richer, our cup runneth over, when we share our richness with others (Hellinger, 2010b).

Marco Moretti and Daniela Poggioli

PART ONE
Theory

Bert Hellinger's Family Constellations

by Marco Moretti

What is it that connects us to the world, to a grain of sand, to the heaven and to a wildflower? What is it that holds us together beyond the limits of space and time? Many philosophers and scientists have tried to answer these questions.

Each answer will lead to a vision that opens new possibilities while excluding others. Nevertheless various human experiences confirm that we are all connected, sometimes inexplicably, to one another.

Family Constellations show these connections. Simply yet profoundly they make the invisible visible and the inexplicit explicit – not through verbal narration, but thanks to the visual and experiential representation of the dynamics that occur within a system of relations.

Family Constellations act upon different dimensions of existence, and because of their simplicity and efficacy, respond to the growing demand for fast interventions that bring resolution. That does not mean the solution to family or interpersonal problems is an uncomplicated matter presenting no difficulties. The techniques' simplicity and efficacy consist in the possibility of seeing directly and concretely, in a short time, what happens in the sphere of relationships, what limits us and what hinders us, and how to resolve our interpersonal disharmonies, to gain greater strength, autonomy and serenity.

Sources and techniques

Bert Hellinger, a German psychotherapist, like most great innovators, has an eclectic background, which in his case spans psychoanalysis and systemic therapy (Hellinger *et al.*, 2005). He was born Johann Anton Hellinger in Leimen, Germany, in 1925, into a Catholic family. In 1942 he enlisted in the German army and fought on the Western front. After the Second World War he began a religious training that led him to ordain as a priest in the Catholic Church. He studied Philosophy and Theology at the University of Würzburg, and in 1952 became priest of the *Kongregation der Mariannhiller Missionare*, where he received the name Suitbert, later shortened to Bert. The same year he was transferred to South Africa as a missionary, and for 16 years carried out his parochial service. He continued his studies at the University of Pietermaritzburg and the University of South Africa, graduating in Humanistic Sciences. While undertaking his pastoral service, he started a career as teacher in a school for Zulu children.

At the end of the 60's, during an ecumenical and multiracial course with a phenomenological bent, one of the leaders asked the group: "What is more important to you: your ideals or people? What would you choose to sacrifice or save?" (Weber, 1993). After this question Hellinger spent a sleepless night that led him to reconsider his position in the Church and to direct his work towards people. Being a parish priest was limiting his potential for personal growth and for helping others. Recalling this episode later, Hellinger says: "A good question can really be precious" (Weber, 1993).

In 1968 he returned to Germany where he met his first wife Herta. In that period he attended a Gestalt Therapy workshop led by Ruth Cohn and Hilarion Petzold. Of this experience Hellinger was to say: "Ruth Cohn did fantastic work with me. With her help I looked to my future. In that session it was clear to me that I wanted to leave the order and get married. She made me turn to the group and say: "I'm leaving". It was very moving" (Hellinger *et al.*, 2005). Thus in 1971 he renounced his clerical status, married Herta, and moved to Vienna where he undertook psychoanalytic training at the *Wiener Arbeitskreis für Tiefenpsychologie* which in 1982 was recognized by the *Münchner Arbeitsgemeinschaft für Psychoanalyse* in Germany.

In 1973 Hellinger, tireless in his ongoing personal training, moved to the United States for nine months to study Primal Therapy with Arthur Janov. In that time he met Frank Farrelly and his Provocative Therapy and with Transactional Analysis through Fanita English.

THEORY

With his wife Herta he developed and used for several years a methodological approach in which he integrated Gestalt Therapy, Primal Therapy and Transactional Analysis, and which included work on the body, the emotions and the mind, acknowledging both intra-psychic and interpersonal dynamics.

After reading an article by Jay Haley (1959) about the "perverse triangle" in families of schizophrenic patients – a kind of relationship in which one parent and one child create an intense and preferential relationship to the detriment of the other parent – and the book by Boszormenyi-Nagy: *Invisible Loyalties* (1973), about hidden loyalties and the need for balance, in the family, between giving and taking, he decided to study Systemic Therapy in depth. He attended Lindau's psychotherapy weeks with Thea Schönfelder, thanks to which he gained experience of Virginia Satir's *Family Sculpting* and *Family Reconstruction Technique*. Hellinger was so deeply struck by this technique that he said: "I saw that this was the future" (Hellinger, 2010a). He learned Eriksonian hypnotherapy, Neuro-linguistic Programming, and continued to develop Family Sculpting and Systemic Therapy both with Thea Schönfelder and with Ruth McClendon and Leslie Kadis. From then on Hellinger moved more and more towards a systemic view, uniting in his own way Family Sculpting with his previous experiences.

For many years I offered courses in script analysis developed by Eric Berne, the creator of Transactional Analysis, described in detail in his book: What do you say after you say hello? (1972). He found that we live our life on the basis of a secret plan, as though acting from a script, almost word for word, on the stage of life.

I thought this script was already enacted by another member of our family, and that we simply take it on and re-enact it.

Suddenly I realized it was an entanglement. In our life we are entangled in the destiny of people who have been forgotten or excluded by our family.

Suddenly I saw the mechanism of Family Constellations. During the representations, the representatives bring to light the ones who are excluded and show how we can take them back into the family and into the heart, to the great relief of many.

At the same time, while writing an essay on guilt and innocence within the system, I realized that there exists an original order, which prescribes that whoever arrives first has precedence over those who come later (Hellinger, 2010a).

In the 80's Hellinger discovered some important laws that govern the family system, the Orders of Love, and began to develop the Family Constellations technique, which he would present to the public with the text, edited by Gunthard Weber (1993), *Zweierlei Glück. Die systemische Psychotherapie Bert Hellingers*. The book was so successful

THEORY

that in 1994 Hellinger started running public workshops in which more and more people participated.

In that period Hellinger started training his first students and collaborators. His marriage to Herta went into crisis after several years, and following the divorce, Hellinger married, in 2005, his collaborator Maria Sophie, who is to this day his right hand in both the running of seminars and Family Constellations training.

From 1994 to today the Family Constellations have continued to evolve. In broad terms, the technique originally adopted is:

1. A group of people form a big circle or semicircle in the presence of the leader.
2. The leader asks who would like to work on herself.
3. The client stands next to the leader, who asks her what she would like to work on.
4. The client presents her problem.
5. The leader asks a few questions to help the client focus concretely on the problem and her goal. They agree on a representation, for example to stage the family of origin.
6. The client chooses people from the group to represent the components of her family, including herself, and arranges them in space as she pictures them in relationship.
7. The representatives stand in silence, listening to their sensations and feelings.

8. The leader may ask the client and representatives questions about how they are feeling and what they are experiencing.
9. The leader may choose to have them speak a word or sentence to another representative, and may also choose to shift members' positions. He may also at any point choose to replace the person representing the client with the client herself.
10. The performance ends when the leader finds a solution in which the client and all the actors feel right and in harmony with one another.

In the 90's Hellinger worked with the Constellations structurally, keeping in mind the hierarchical aspects of the family system, intervening in the representation by relocating the representatives in a different relationship – the Orders of Love that he identified – and by making one of them say a ritual sentence that would allow them to adapt to the new order. The approach aims at the solution of the client's problem, and the representation ends when the new image, and resolution, is achieved.

After the client has staged the representatives, she was asked how she feels. Generally she was impressed by the result because it was different to how she had imagined it. The representatives were asked how they felt. Changes were then made till everyone felt well. Often extra representatives were

THEORY

added. [...] The attention during the representations was on the current family or on the original one. [...] This methodology was regarded to be a deepening of the psychotherapy and remained more or less restricted to this sphere (Hellinger, 2010a).

So my idea was: a family with problems looks for the most suitable order. We would find it during the representation. It showed in the wellbeing of all the representatives. I would then make the client say sentences which allowed the inner adaptation to the newly recognized order and which helped her to undo an entanglement. For example, a phrase such as: "Now I am staying", "I am here for you now", or – if a person had rejected her mother – "I now honor you", "I accept what you give me". In this way you touch something in the soul. Reconciliation happened though a hug. Sometimes it is part of the order for the client to withdraw. The representations of the Family Constellations done in this way are great work: you see this from their effect (Hellinger, 2005).

Towards the end of the 90's Hellinger began more and more to understand the power of the Knowing Field (see chapter 2), and how the representatives of the family actually felt like the people they were representing.

Hellinger became more and more "essential" in his choice of what to stage, and left more room for the movement of the representatives. He went along with those spontaneous movements he first called "movements of the soul" and later called "movements of the Spirit". This new approach was not oriented to the solution of the problem, but to the movement of the soul: the representation ended when it moved in the direction of healing.

At a later stage I rarely asked the representatives how they were feeling. Instead of the whole family, I would often choose only one representative for the client. It was important that the representative, without knowing anything about the client, went along with the inner movement, as she would take possession of her from the inside outward. I would no longer ask questions about her sensations, expectations, and fears. The performance had no goal predetermined by the client, and the leader did not place himself at her service. All was left to the movements, as they took the representative, beyond any idea of problem and solution, and beyond psychotherapy as it was understood up to that moment.
Suddenly would come to light what was really happening to the representatives when they felt led by a force other than their own. They felt like mediators, taken and moved by another force. The leader too would follow these movements: he too would let himself be taken and guided by them (Hellinger, 2010a).

Today [2005] I often represent only one person – often the client herself and not a representative. With enough time, something develops through a movement. Her movements show how the whole system seeks and finds a solution. All you must do is observe the movements to see what the system needs. The family field manifests itself through that one person, without the need to stage representatives for all the family members. The field acts through that one person. [...] Then perhaps you can add representatives, and from the whole you see what is essential for the system. You do not represent the solution, but only the movement necessary for resolving something. As soon as the decisive movement starts, I may interrupt (Hellinger, 2005).

From 2000 on Hellinger used more and more the scope of the Spiritual Consciousness in the representations, and he changed his intervention in a more spiritual direction, using the fewest, essential words. This new technique, from 2007 on, he called Spiritual Family Constellations.

Since 2012 Hellinger has spoken of Mediumistic Family Constellations. Mediumistic Constellations use almost no words and the leader's intervention is almost entirely on a spiritual plane. The leader and the group become something like a "channel" at the service of the Spiritual Consciousness: they let themselves be taken by, and they submit to, the force of the Spirit that is trying to manifest itself in the Field, and they work on this level of consciousness.

You depart from the "mediumistic" dimension when you ask a client what is her wish. The leader will seek a solution that permits her to realize this wish. [...] The same occurs for the representatives. They too will try to satisfy the client's wish. They will allow themselves to be guided by it instead of by the inner movement that had taken them from the beginning.

[...] [In the Mediumistic Constellations] often the facilitator – in this case myself, Bert Hellinger – does not even look at the client sitting next to him. He asks her to close her eyes; and he closes his eyes too. He goes deep inside himself and waits for a suggestion from another dimension. Suddenly a sentence arises – sometimes it is just a word – without his understanding its meaning. He communicates this sentence or word to the client, and asks her to repeat it or say it to someone inside herself. Suddenly the client is taken by a movement that sets in motion something essential. Many participants have the same experience. They too are taken by an inner movement that allows them to complete something of the past, and that makes necessary something new.

[...] After one of these sentences has had its effect, the facilitator asks the client how she feels and whether this phrase is sufficient. Often the client answers yes to this question. She stands up and returns to her place, without the facilitator asking her what her goal was.

[...] If the client expresses a further wish, the facilitator starts a representation if he is inwardly moved to do so. He places someone in the scene – either the client or a representative. Or else he chooses a representative for another person belonging to the system, usually without expressly pointing her out.

[...] At the end of the representation all members of the family or of the group involved feel mutual love and respect. A

THEORY

Mediumistic Constellation can overcome that which divides. Sometimes the representations also transform into a peace movement between peoples. And these movements often irresistibly involve all members of a group. Here the movement is the work of a different awareness and a different world. (Hellinger, 2013).

The evolution of the technique continues to this day with the New Family Constellations in which: "The solution, the healing and the peace is in the whole group" (www2.hellinger.com).

Today various therapists and facilitators use the technique of Family Constellations in one of the forms developed by Hellinger. Generally, this technique is defined as "Systemic Constellations", since it is applied not only to family systems but to all systems, whether they be biological (bodily aspects, organs, pathologies, physical symptoms, etc.), intra-psychic (inner parts or subpersonalities, attitudes, sensations, emotions, desires, etc.), relational (interpersonal or sexual problems, affective choices, conflicts, heredity, moves, etc.), work-related (professional or organizational problems, etc.), social (marginalization, ethnic or political conflict, difficulty integrating, etc.), or spiritual (spiritual obstacles of various kinds, spiritual growth, relationship with God, etc.). In our text we use the term "Family Constellations", seeing as Hellinger himself continues to use it, even though it is in fact a technique applicable to any kind of relation.

Bert Hellinger's Family Constellations

The technique of Family Constellations owes much to various therapeutic and philosophical approaches that Hellinger has made his own:

- From Phenomenology, the understanding of the other and her experience, through observation and description of what happens, as well as of how it is manifested.
- From Transpersonal Psychology, the spiritual dimension of the human being.
- From Psychoanalysis, attention to the link between intra-psychic dynamics and family relations.
- From Primal Therapy, bodywork on movement and the original emotions we experience, after birth, towards our parents.
- From Gestalt Therapy, attention to the totality in its form, and the therapeutic experience in the here and now.
- From Transactional Analysis, attention to life scripts and the resolving sentences that allow one to be free of them.
- From Eriksonian Therapy and Neuro-linguistic Programming, attention to nonverbal communication, to all the body's signals, and to use of language (from prosody to metaphor).
- From Systemic-Relational Therapy, the conception of the family as a system in which each member is in interdependent relation with the others, and every event,

emotion, symptom and behavior has relational significance.

From Systemic-Relational Therapy, the main contributions come from:

1. Virginia Satir, for attention given to harmony and to the whole of existence (wholistic approach) and, above all, for the *Family Sculpting* and the *Family Reconstruction Technique*, where the client, as in Family Constellations, chooses some members of the group and places them in scene to represent her own family, with a view to understanding the family dynamics (Satir, 1967; Satir and Baldwin, 1983; Satir, 1988).
2. Ivan Boszormenyi-Nagy, for the concept of *balance of fairness*, in other words, the balance of give and take in a family, and the concept of *loyalties*, visible and invisible, which bind the family members between current and previous generations (Boszormenyi-Nagy and Spark, 1973).
3. Jay Haley, for the *hierarchical* and *normative* model within the family, in other words, the family's hierarchical structure, which can be considered "correct" when it does not produce pathology, and which the therapist can reorganize when it is unbalanced, by using strategic solutions (Haley, 1959; Haley, 1976).

What are the Family Constellations' original contributions?

- The recognition and possibility of working with and through a Knowing Field, which, during the representations, allows the family dynamics, with all their limits and potentialities, to emerge.
- The recognition and possibility of working on three different planes of consciousness: Personal, Collective and Spiritual.
- The recognition of certain systemic laws tied to belonging, guilt and innocence, give and take, the various forms of compensation, and the Orders of Love.
- The concrete demonstration of loyalty ties, forms of entanglement and, in general, dependence on previous generations, but above all how all this limits and at the same time heals when brought to light.

The Knowing Field

by Marco Moretti

What distinguishes the Family Constellations technique from other psychological techniques is the use of the "Knowing Field". Anyone who has participated in Family Constellations workshop groups has experienced this phenomenon in which the representatives feel and have physical conditions, sensations, emotions, states of mind, and mental images that belong to the subject represented.

> *Suddenly the representatives feel like the people they represent without knowing anything about them. Thus what happens during the representations of family constellations is linked to a more encompassing whole, a field of consciousness in which all members of the family are present and all are in resonance with all the others (Hellinger, 2008).*

This phenomenon had already been observed by family therapists of the past. Virgina Satir (1967), for example, reports an experience in which Gregory Bateson and his collaborators, who were working in Palo Alto in 1954, found to their astonishment, while trying to demonstrate certain family dynamics through a *simulated family*, that in impersonating the members of a family, they had very intense feelings in the role and the behaviors they were representing. Satir reports other experiences of this kind:

> *On one memorable occasion, a young social worker played the identified-patient daughter in a particular simulated family, while a general physician, interested in family therapy, was her simulated father. At the end of about forty minutes of family interaction, the "daughter" stood up, threw her arms around the older man and stated, "I really love you!" and he, with tears streaming down his face, stated, "It's the first time I have ever really felt what I missed in not having a daughter" (Satir, 1967).*

The American physicist Joseph Henry says: "The seeds of great discoveries are constantly floating around us, but they only take root in minds well-prepared to receive them" (Rosenman, 1988). The "Knowing Field" existed before Hellinger intuited its therapeutic capacity. Unlike his predecessors, Hellinger recognized its value and used it amply in the Family Constellations.

The fact that a representative can gain access to the information belonging to the family system or other interpersonal systems is an essential peculiarity of the Knowing Field.

George, a client of mine, has for some time been unable to communicate adequately with a friend. During an Individual

Constellation, while he was impersonating his friend, he found himself gripped by severe anxiety. I help him to let himself be guided by this state of mind and suddenly George sees the image of a woman, who is not the friend's wife, and realizes the friend is having an extramarital affair that is complicating his life. At that moment the anxiety vanishes. Actually the friend has never confided this to George; nevertheless George decides to trust the intuition.

George understands his friend's anxiety and from that moment relates to him differently, more empathically. After a few days he finds his intuition confirmed by fact: the friend really is having an extramarital relationship that is complicating his life. He would have wanted to speak about it with George, but till that moment had not the courage to do so. In a sense the Individual Constellation has allowed George and his friend to overcome the impasse.

The Knowing Field manifests this information through phenomena of energetic "resonance"; yet the Family Constellations must not be seen as a tool for use in investigating the truth of occurrences.

In a female participant's constellation, the representative had the distinct sensation that she had been raped by her father. The representative of the father confirmed this. However, after the representation, the representative denied ever having been sexually abused.

THEORY

Two weeks later my colleague received a phone call from the participant. She had gone to see her sister and told her about the representation. Suddenly the sister burst out crying and admitted she had been raped by their father.
I concluded that in the family the energy of sexual abuse was present. [...] Thus in the constellations we effectively find the truth, but not necessarily an effective truth (Ulsamer, 2001).

The term "Knowing Field" was coined by Albrecht Mahr (1999), psychoanalyst and psychotherapist, colleague of Bert Hellinger. An analogous term is "Morphic Field" or "Morphogenetic Field", coined by Rupert Sheldrake (1981), biochemist and philosopher of science, to hypothesize the existence of "Fields" organizing everything that exists – from atoms to multicellular organisms – to take form and learn through mechanisms of "morphic resonance". Sheldrake believes the "morphic resonance" works as a transmitter of information between organisms of the same species, even when they are not in physical contact with one another.

This phenomenon calls to mind that of quantum *entanglement*, in which two elementary particles, part of the same molecular system that are then separated, stay connected independently of space and time, and mutually and instantaneously influence each other however far apart they are. This quantum phenomenon led the physicist David Bohm (1980) to hypothesize that the universe was like a hologram in each single part of which it is possible to find the whole. According to Bohm, what we perceive is the manifestation ("explicate order") of an "implicate order" that exists beyond the space-time dimension and that connects everything.

Already Carl Gustav Jung (1952), the famous Swiss psychiatrist and psychoanalyst, in collaboration with the physicist Wolfgang Pauli, had formulated his idea of "synchronicity" to explain the contemporaneity of two or more events connected meaningfully but not causally. For Jung the phenomenon of synchronicity was evidence of the so-called "collective unconscious", the collective psyche shared unconsciously by all humanity.

> Several times I have found, both in group and individual Family Constellations workshops, that in the middle of the representation a phone call would come from one of the represented subjects not physically present in the context. Among these I recall a touching episode one Sunday afternoon. The whole group was struck when it discovered, straight after deep work on the relationship between mother and daughter, that from San Francisco the daughter had called the mother in Italy, despite a time-difference of nine hours, at the exact moment we were witnessing a heart-to-heart encounter. The daughter rarely called and did not know that the mother was participating that day in a Family Constellations workshop.

THEORY

Even in ancient times they spoke of a collective psyche, the *Anima Mundi*. Thus Plato described the world as a real living being equipped with soul and intelligence. And while in 1952, thanks to Carl Jung, "synchronicity" was offered as evidence for a "collective unconscious", it is only in these last years, thanks to Bert Hellinger, that we know how to work directly with this collective psyche through the Knowing Field.

In contrast to other methods, which work mainly on individuals or relations between them, the Family Constellations work specifically with and through the Knowing Field. The technique consists in entering into contact with this Field, to bring out deep dynamics of the represented system, and, with the guidance of the Field's energy, to reach solutions that will bring about greater systemic harmony. If the work is done in depth, that is, in deep contact with the Knowing Field, the changes occur in two ways:

1. The client changes his own representation of reality.
2. The Knowing Field undergoes a restructuring that is transferred by "morphic resonance" to the family or interpersonal system.

The changes occur when the therapist is able to work with the Knowing Field so that what happens is what is somehow already trying to happen. When they occur, the changes are in fact the possible ones, and in a way those that are "wanted" by the family or interpersonal system.

If it be true that certain people are specially gifted in the art of acting upon complex systems with homeostatic or ecological characteristics, and that these people do not operate by spelling out the interaction of all relevant variables, then these people must use some inner ecology of ideas as an analogic model. (By "ideas" I mean thoughts, premises, affects, perceptions of self, etc.) But if this skill is, in some sense, really an "art" then it is possible that the inner "ecology of ideas" is a close synonym of what might also be called aesthetic sensibility (Bateson, 1991).

Bateson describes the ability to act on living systems as an "aesthetic sensibility", a sensitivity to the "pattern that connects". Because of his sensitivity to the Knowing Field – consisting in a profound listening and respect – the therapist can help the client listen to what is trying to occur in the family system to make for greater systemic harmony. By "deep listening" I mean a facilitator's capacity to observe and feel empathically what is happening, moment by moment, in the whole space of the representation, while trusting his own perceptions. By "respect" I mean the attitude of placing oneself at the last position of the family or interpersonal system, given that the therapist is the last to arrive and is at the service of what is trying to manifest in the Field. It is up to the therapist's experience to know how to decode and follow what is happening in the Knowing Field, to enhance any such movement in the direction of greater harmony.

> Giuseppina, a client of mine, is a single mother who left her work after the birth of her child. The job had always given her great satisfaction, but she sacrificed it willingly to be with her little daughter. Now that the daughter is eighteen months' old, Giuseppina wants to go back to work, but at the same time she is afraid she'll be neglecting her child.
> In the Individual Constellation we stage her, her job, and her daughter. The job, which is creative and which takes place in nature, is full of life and wants to meet Giuseppina again. She is in anguish and is tending to distance herself from the job. The daughter, placed between the mother and the job, is joyous when the mother is near the job, and sad when she moves away from it. The job also grows sad at the distancing. When Giuseppina moves away from the job her anguish lessens, but she attempts a suffocating contact with the daughter that makes the child, in turn, distance herself from her mother. Listening to the field, I perceive harmony, joy and vitality when the mother and the job are close. The child also feels happier and in the right place – at the right distance from the mother. If, however, the mother distances herself from the job, she

calms her anguish, but the system tends to disintegrate and lose energy and vitality.

My function is to help Giuseppina have awareness of these qualitative differences and manage her anguish while respecting the whole system. Now Giuseppina is aware that going back to work means greater happiness for all, and that she can face the anxiety by finding organizational strategies that allow her to manage her profession and her family in daily life.

A few days later Giuseppina receives an interesting offer from her employer, who had not been in touch for a long time, that makes her very happy. Giuseppina goes to the workplace with her daughter, telling her what it is all about, and both are exceptionally joyful.

Planes of Consciousness

During his experience with Family Constellations Hellinger realized that in the Knowing Field, during the representations, at least three different planes of consciousness come to be manifest: personal, collective and spiritual.

These planes of consciousness are part of the personal, collective, and spiritual or transpersonal unconscious. By "unconscious" I mean the set of all the independent psychic activity that takes place in us and outside of us, from the biological plane to the mental and spiritual one. By "consciousness" I mean the part of psychic activity that explicitly manifests itself.

The personal consciousness is the conscious aspect of the individual; the collective consciousness is the explicit manifestation of the collective unconscious (to which belong the psychic dynamics of the family, community, nation, race, humanity, animal and biological realm); the spiritual consciousness is the explicit manifestation of the spiritual or transpersonal unconscious (seat of the Spirit's energies, to which belong the spiritual, ethical and creative expressions).

We are inextricably linked and in continuous reciprocal contact, not only socially or on the physical plane, but also because of the exchange that continually occurs between our thoughts, feelings, and those of others. We are part of a whole like the cells of our bodies, each distinct yet at the same time an integral part of a wider human group (Assagioli, 1996).

The diagram in figure 1 shows the various psychic planes in which we human beings live. It was originally conceived by Carl Gustav Jung. I have modified it in this text, according to Bert Hellinger's observations and Roberto Assagioli's studies, and have included in it the spiritual dimension represented by the spiritual unconscious and by the Spirit. The planes are not neatly separated from one another, as continuous processes of "psychic osmosis" occur between them.

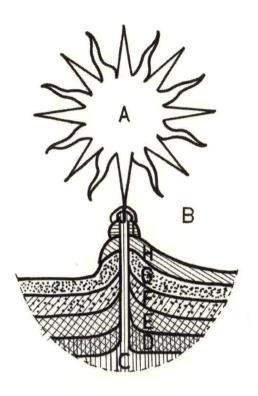

Figure 1 (Jacobi, 1942; Assagioli, 1965, 2007)

A – Spirit. B – Spiritual Unconscious.
C – Biological Realm. D – Animal Kingdom.
E – Humanity. F – Race. G – Nation. H – Community.
I – Family. J – Individual

The personal consciousness concerns the individual sphere. It is the part of the individual that is to some extent conscious of itself and that bases its choices on its own needs, compulsions, desires, ideals, volitions and morality, all in relation to oneself, the family and the group to which one belongs. Counseling and psychotherapy is largely directed at this plane of consciousness.

The personal consciousness, in its moral aspect, responds with wellbeing or disease according to the degree to which one's desires, thoughts, choices and actions correspond to the familial and social expectations, and to the balance between give and take. It is separatist, egocentric, conservative, and keeps the individual tied to his vital context, the family and the group, to the exclusion of all else, or even against other groups and family systems. This kind of consciousness acts from feelings of loyalty and the need for balance, and has the aim of guaranteeing the individual's survival in the context to which he belongs.

> *This consciousness was extremely important when we were children. Children do all they can to guarantee their belonging, because without it they would be lost. The personal consciousness assures survival in the group and among the people who can guarantee it (Hellinger, 2008).*

It is the personal consciousness that generated Giuseppina's fear, her sense of guilt at the idea of resuming work and neglecting her child, and the anguish at not being able to reconcile her wish with the social expectations about the mother-child bond. Giuseppina found her wellbeing when she saw that the cohesion of the family system and the sense of belonging were not in danger if she pursued her wish. Thus she could justify doing so. If Giuseppina had pursued her desire at the cost of the bond with her child, her personal consciousness would probably have required of her some form of atonement to compensate the injustice.

Many clients come for consultation complaining and reproaching themselves or someone else for their problems. An Individual Constellation can "detach" the client from his usual descriptions of the problem and help him consider the situation from other points of view – not to assign blame, but to understand "what happened and what bond of love, often blind, may show up in the client's problem" (Schneider and Schneider, 2006).

> Claudia, a client of mine, at last gets the job she has always dreamed of, but cannot carry it out. She feels blocked. In the Individual Constellation we place the job in the scene. The job starts to feel itself pulled downwards, the knees bend and the body goes to kneeling position. I ask her before whom she is kneeling: it is her father, who died a few years before. I thus make the woman lie down and impersonate her father. He feels sad because his daughter is angry with him and does not honor him. He acknowledges having been an absent father, even if he did try his best to help his daughter finish her studies so she could get that job she wanted very much. I therefore ask the woman to stand up and take her position. Claudia is now facing her dead father and her job, kneeling beside him. She is

very resentful. She acknowledges that it is thanks to her father she managed to obtain the job, but she does not feel like thanking him. Thus the job remains kneeling in Claudia's place.

Claudia's personal consciousness stopped her from carrying out her job successfully. To have success, she would have had to thank her father. This is an atonement that seeks to compensate for the ingratitude regarding what she received. The dynamics of compensation avoid facing responsibility, injustice or anything else that has compromised the balance of give and take and the sense of belonging. These dynamics can even make members of the family become ill or die, just for the sake of re-balancing the system. That usually happens in cases where grave injustice is committed within the family. Such dynamics are not capable of resolving the problems they try to compensate. Rather, the solution is to recognize sincerely one's own responsibility, or what is due, and to assume it before the rest of the family or in a Family Constellation. When this is done with sincerity and emotional involvement, the family system finds harmony and peace.

The collective consciousness is more inclusive than the personal one and comprises the dynamics of the family, community, nation, race, and of humanity. This consciousness serves the survival of the system (family, group, or wider still) even though it demands the sacrifice of single individuals, and responds to the laws of the Orders of Love and of belonging. It safeguards the order and completeness of the family, group, or wider systems, and does so by reintroducing excluded members, victims and perpetrators.

To what must we pay attention during the representations of the family constellations as far as the collective consciousness is concerned?

First, we must not exclude any member of our family or the client's family. Furthermore, it is necessary to find the excluded members, to look at them and welcome them with love. We will succeed in this only if we have left behind the distinction between good and bad, and if we also consider the children who have never been born, difficult though that may be. It requires courage and clarity.

Second, we must respect the hierarchy. This means first that the help we give makes us temporarily members of the client's family. But we are the last arrivals in the family, so we have last place.

[...] Violation of the hierarchy can sometimes endanger life itself, for example, if the client has taken on a responsibility that, according to the hierarchy, is his parents' and not his. In this case he sometimes inwardly says to his parents: "I in your place".

The violation of the hierarchy can also be dangerous for the facilitator, for instance when he expects to take on something that is only up to the client. In this case he raises himself above the client, who in turn does this in relation to her parents, and as the facilitator perhaps did as a child. However it happens above all when the facilitator believes he can change the client's destiny or protect her from it (Hellinger, 2008).

A married woman, a client of mine called Lucia, has for some time suffered from a deep feeling of exclusion in both her family and work circles. In the Individual Constellation we decide to represent the source of this sense of exclusion. Lucia enters deeply into this state of mind, its sensations and emotions. At a certain point an image appears: it is of a woman shut in a room and tied to a bed. I ask her to shift into the image of this woman and to represent her. Lucia starts to suffer physically. She feels she is the beaten and undernourished woman whom her sisters have locked in this dark room. This woman demands her dignity. I then ask her to move out of that position and into the image of the sister who made the decision. This woman is so full of hate and envy as to manipulate the family into excluding her younger sister, who is much more beautiful and intelligent than she is. I ask Lucia to leave that position and enter herself. Now Lucia sees the source of her sense of exclusion and the fact that it was entangled with the excluded woman. She feels like bowing and honoring this woman with love. She feels her value, dignity, and belonging to the family must all be acknowledged. Suddenly Lucia has a memory and recognizes the woman to be a sister of her maternal grandmother. Now everything has fallen into place and Lucia has freed herself of the sense of exclusion.

The collective consciousness, based on the law of belonging, required that the excluded woman be reintegrated. Thus one of her descendants, Lucia, took on the sense of exclusion through entanglement with her great-aunt.

The psychological rule says that when an inner situation is not made conscious, it happens outside, as fate (Jung, 1951).

This psychological rule can be translated, in a systemic-relational sense, in this way: "When a family member is not recognized or excluded, his peculiarities reappear in the family's future as fate".

The family is like a living organism that, while gradually replacing its members, maintains its consciousness through time: therefore, if today a family member is excluded, he will return in future as the destiny of one of his descendants. Thanks to the Family Constellations it is possible to become aware of these dynamics, restore what has been removed and give back to the family system the harmony that is its due.

The spiritual consciousness is the most inclusive of them all: it is the sense of the eternal and the transcendent, through which is manifest love of the Spirit. Love of the Spirit has no limits and embraces all beings as part of the same Reality: "[...] for he maketh his sun to rise on the evil and on the good, and sendeth rain on the just and on the unjust" (Holy Bible: Matthew 5, 45). Spiritual consciousness is benevolent and understanding towards all, it is not tied to the common moral sense, and it expresses ethical values of a universal kind. Its highest manifestation is Agape, unconditional love. Its goal is to heal and transcend all limits and divisions created by separative and antagonistic statements, to realize a nobler and vaster life consisting of peace, love and joy. All then appears transfigured in the aura of Spirit, in which is perceived the throb of Unity (Assagioli 1965; 2007).

Gregory Bateson states that the sacred is related to the beautiful (Bateson, 1979) and that

> *The damage is the taking apart. The sacredness is the coming together. The sacred is the hook up, the total hook up and not the product of the split (Bateson, 1991).*

Spiritual consciousness is manifest during the representations when the leader and participants are inwardly absorbed and completely open: without aims, without wanting explanations, without fear of what might manifest itself, and are receptive to the movements that tend to happen by themselves. These are very slow movements that shift the Constellation in such a harmonious way that people are left spellbound; they then perceive a moving sense of elevation and become aware that something sacred is happening. They are movements that move the representatives from the outside, but come from the most inner and elevated part of consciousness: the soul. Therefore, in the early stages, Hellinger called them "movements of the soul", but later, perceiving them to be linked to the force of Spirit, preferred to call them "movements of the Spirit".

Suddenly [the representatives] are seized by a movement, without being able to guide it in any way. [...] The people feel in harmony with a movement that sets something in motion through them. [...] As soon as personal aims come into play, such as helping someone, or fear of what may come to light and where it might lead, the relationship with the Spirit is interrupted. The absorption is lost. For instance people become restless. [...] When someone moves abruptly it means she is moved by an aim and is no longer in tune with the movements of the Spirit. She is no longer in absorption, no longer reliable, and must be replaced by another representative.
It is above all the leader of the Constellation that must renounce all aims and interpretations. He too is taken by movements of the Spirit. Therefore he acts only when he feels impelled by them to carry out a further step or to say a sentence, which he expresses directly, or makes a representative express. [...] The leader is at the service of the Spirit's movements and he goes along with them. [...] Where do these movements lead? They unite what was previously

divided. They are always movements of love. [...] A healing movement (Hellinger 2008).

[...] Every truly productive and creative act, takes place in a collected mind, in silence, in the inner regions of the soul (Assagioli, 1922).

Every efficacious and creative action happens from high to low and from inside to outside; that is, from the highest point we can reach internally (Assagioli, 1967).

It is mainly the leader who must be in "tune", as it were, with the spiritual consciousness and the love of the Spirit, to be in harmony with the Spirit's movements and healing. In other words he must be open to all participants – and the whole system represented – with the same love: Agape, unconditional love. This kind of love has no preference for one person rather than another. If the leader inwardly tends to judge a member of the family, he distances himself from the spiritual consciousness and is no longer able to go along with movements of the Spirit. By the same token, he also distances himself if he feels more compassion for one rather than another. The leader is in "tune" with the spiritual consciousness when he can embrace the whole system and all that happens in it, just as it is, with the same empathy and benevolence.

The Knowing Field

Ilaria, a client of mine, has always had a terrible relationship with her daughter. She had her when she was just fifteen years' old, and it was the grandmother who always looked after the child. Now Ilaria would like to mend their relationship, but the daughter doesn't want to know about it. So the mother consults me for an Individual Constellation. We decide to represent the two of them, facing each other. I place her in the position of the daughter. She listens to her sensations and her emotions, and perceives a strong closure in her heart: she feels hate for her mother, feels that the mother wants to come closer to her, but she does not want to know. I then place her in the position of mother, facing the daughter. She is sorry about what the daughter feels, but is aware of her own wrongs, of the fact that the grandmother took care of her daughter. She would like to draw closer to her daughter but out of respect she holds back from doing so.

Despite the real difficulties that I observe, I perceive in my heart a feeling of peace, so I decide to listen to this peace and breathe into it. After a while I feel like suggesting to the mother to stand still, in front of her daughter, and to look at her with love. We stay still for a few minutes. Ilaria looks at her daughter with love and in this peace I breathe. I perceive this peace expanding ever more. I then feel it's right to place the mother in the daughter's position, facing the mother. And I tell her simply to look at her mother. We stay quiet and still for a few minutes and I feel inside me a deep love, besides the peace. I keep breathing and stay open, observing and listening to what takes place before me. Suddenly the daughter bursts into tears: the pain of her whole life is pouring into her tears.

THEORY

In that moment, I feel that the love I had begun to perceive explodes and flares up in ever-wider waves and embraces the whole room. The daughter is transfigured into a little child and feels a heart-rending desire to be taken into her mother's arms. Now the movement that had been interrupted years ago can be concluded. I tell her to imagine being taken in her mother's arms, and I let her stay in that position till she feels at peace, till I feel she is completely "nourished" by maternal love. Afterwards I place the woman in the position of mother and ask her to imagine holding her daughter in her arms. I leave her there for some minutes, and give her time to express all her love. At the end of the Constellation, we both feel a sense of the sacred and a wish to stay in silence, in contact with the love of the Spirit.

It is hard to describe what one experiences when the spiritual consciousness is manifest in a Constellation. Obviously the rational mind demands an explanation, but at the end of a spiritually poignant Constellation, it is better to remain in silence so as not to dissipate the spiritual energies that have been tapped and collected. After a reasonable time it is possible to answer the client's questions. In Ilaria's case: "What should I do with my daughter?", "Should I meet her?", "Can I speak with her about what happened today?", "Is what happened a fantasy of mine?", "What should I expect when I go home?", and so on. The therapist's experience and his capacity to stay in touch with the spiritual consciousness are essential elements in helping the client to understand and find her bearings in her everyday life.

When the rational mind steps in after a Constellation of this kind, the client loses contact with the spiritual consciousness and in doing so tends to force the therapist to detach himself from it too. However the therapist can continue to be centered, while responding empathically to the client without losing touch with the spiritual consciousness: it's a matter of experience. Thus the client rediscovers her confidence and feels that everything will go as it should.

During the Constellations the three different planes of consciousness – personal, collective and spiritual – can manifest with greater or lesser intensity and simultaneous presence. The therapist must recognize them, because each one has different goals, a different way of manifesting itself, and they are often in conflict with one another.

The phenomenological approach that characterizes the Family Constellations suggests that we work with what presents itself, just as it is, without the therapist trying to direct the process according to his aims. If a certain plane of consciousness emerges, the therapist works with that, bearing in mind the other two. Why must the therapist bear in mind the other planes anyway? Because often the problems that arise on one plane can be overcome only by transcending that plane of consciousness, as happened with Ilaria.

Each plane of consciousness has a wider range, thus even among them a hierarchical order is in force: at the highest place is the spiritual consciousness, then the collective, and last the personal. When these planes of consciousness are considered in their order and the therapist serves them while standing at the lowest place, the healing movement and love of the Spirit can manifest.

Orders of Love and of Helping
by Marco Moretti and Daniela Poggioli

A disciple asks his teacher: "Tell me what is freedom!".
"Which freedom?" asks the teacher.
"The first freedom is stubbornness. It is like a horse that throws its rider with a triumphant neighing. But all the tighter will it feel his rider's grip later."
"The second freedom is remorse. It is like a helmsman who, after a shipwreck, prefers to stay on the wreck rather than climb onto the lifeboat."
"The third freedom is understanding. It comes after stubbornness and after remorse. It is like a blade of grass that bows to the wind, and as it bows where it is weakest, it resists."
The disciple asked: "Is that all?".
The teacher said: "Many think they are seeking the truth of their soul, but it is the great soul that thinks and seeks through them. Nature can allow a great variety of mistakes, and it habitually and effortlessly replaces false players with new ones. But to anyone who lets the great soul think through him, it concedes in exchange a little freedom; and like a river does with a swimmer who lets himself be taken by the current, it takes him to new shores" (Hellinger, 1998).

Anyone who wishes for freedom and limitless progress, may, as often happens these days, be troubled by concepts such as bond and responsibility. Even before Hellinger, many therapists and scholars of family dynamics had developed methods and techniques for improving and healing the suffering of families, but Hellinger's merit is in his phenomenological way of proceeding, which places the process of perception in the foreground. The "basic orders", the laws that govern living systems and family systems, were discovered and identified after years of observation and experience with Family Constellations, and all can find them in their work with the Constellations. Hellinger calls them "Orders of Love".

To understand the relationship between Order and Love, Hellinger gives the example of a flowing river: the water is the love, the bed of the river is the order. It is love that nourishes and gives life, but it cannot flow unless an order contains and directs it. A life without love is arid, a love without order makes you ill. You receive love and you give it. If this flow of love is regulated and ordered, it nourishes life and promotes growth.

> *Order precedes love, and love can only be developed on the basis of order. Order is primary. If you reverse this relationship and try to transform order through love, you are destined to fail. It doesn't work like that. Love is subordinate to order; afterwards it can grow: just as the seed is subordinate to the ground, where it grows and flowers (Hellinger, 1998).*

Orders of Love and of Helping

There are three main Orders of Love belonging to human systems:

1. Right to belong.
2. Hierarchical structure.
3. Balance between give and take.

Right to belong

The first Order of Love is:

Each member of the group has the same right of belonging. When a member is excluded, for whatever reason, another member will in the future represent the excluded member (Hellinger, 2008).

All who are part of the family system have their unalienable place and therefore must be acknowledged, welcomed and honored.

The systemic operators know this principle but do not always know the consequences. What happens when a person is excluded, marginalized or not acknowledged by the other members of the family? When a family member's right to belong is refused, a disorder arises and extends to later generations.

THEORY

It still commonly happens in families that someone is excluded or harmed in his psychophysical wholeness. In the Family Constellations we have observed some important effects, where the personal and the collective consciousness come into play. As described in the previous chapter, these planes of consciousness are indivisible but powerful aspects, since they influence our behavior and thoughts, often beyond our awareness.

The family system is governed by a collective consciousness that often sacrifices the interests of the individual for a functionality inherent to the system.

In the case of a family member being excluded or deliberately forgotten, what happens is that, in the following generations, another component of the family takes on the burden.

> Anna comes to me (Daniela) in an evident state of anguish and with symptoms she declares are due to insomnia: loss of appetite and frequent panic attacks for which she cannot find any meaning. Anna is 42 years' old, married with two young children, has a good relationship with her family and husband, a satisfying job, and sees nothing that should make her feel so poorly.
>
> I get her to relate how these panic attacks arise, when they occur, and what images they evoke for her.
>
> After a few sessions Anna manages to focus on a particularly anguishing image. On returning home, she has a fourth floor

balcony before her front door: She feels the urge to go there and throw herself off it.

I ask her many questions about her relatives and whether any facts, events or dramas can link her to this symptom.

Anna cannot answer this until, during one session, she has a clear and upsetting image involving a maternal great-aunt, who was known to have fallen off a balcony... What Anna did not know was a secret that someone in the family was guarding. Did the great-aunt fall or did she commit suicide?

Encouraged by me, Anna does a more accurate family investigation, and at last an aunt relates to her what really happened: the great-aunt suffered from a grave depression as a result of great grief, and one day several neighbors found her dead on the ground in the courtyard of the building, below her balcony.

For Anna this was a big discovery; she wept during the meeting, but at the same time felt revived, because she could acknowledge a fact that had occurred many years before her birth, and could bring out into the open this great-aunt, who had been forgotten probably out of the relatives' shame and embarrassment.

The panic attacks gave way to great sadness, but also to an evident relief: Anna took the habit of lighting a little candle every evening in before the picture of her great-aunt.

This is a clear example of entanglement, of identification with one who has been forgotten: Anna identified with the great-aunt she had never met and of whose existence she had not even known.

The collective consciousness demands that each person have a place within the family. Belonging guarantees the survival of the group and of the single members, and even if we may think this is no longer necessary given the current state of breakdown in affective and social values, family ties are a firmly-rooted reality in the collective consciousness.

The members of the family that submit to this collective consciousness are the following:

1. *The children: we and our brothers and sisters. Among our brothers and sisters are included dead children and those unborn because of either spontaneous or arranged abortions. These are the very ones we think we can exclude. Naturally children who are hidden or abandoned are also part of the family. Because of the collective consciousness they all have the same right of belonging and are remembered and made present. They are brought back randomly, independently of the subject's wishes or sense of fairness.*
2. *The level above that of the children is made up of the parents and their biological brothers and sisters. Here too, are included all the siblings, just as for the children. The parents' previous partners are also part of the family. If they have been rejected or excluded, and even if they are dead, they will be represented by a child until they are remembered and reintegrated with love.*

3. To the next level belong the grandparents, but without their siblings, unless they have had a special destiny. Their previous partners are also part of this level.
4. Great-grandparents can also be part of the collective consciousness, though this happens rarely. So far I have listed the blood relations, besides the previous partners of parents and grandparents.
5. Furthermore, those whose death and destiny has benefitted the family are also part of the family, for example, if a considerable inheritance has allowed the family to grow rich.
6. Victims of violent acts done by members of the family are also part of our family, above all those who have been killed by members of our family. They too must be seen with love and pain.
7. Now, the last aspect could prove a challenge for some people. If members of our family have been victims of crimes, especially if they have lost their lives, even the killers form part of our family. If they are excluded or rejected, they too will be represented by members of the family under the duress of the collective consciousness (Hellinger, 2008).

Belonging to one family rather than another develops in each person a consciousness made up of values, behaviors, and thoughts that contribute to the formation of one's personality and to one's representation of reality.

The real forces that maintain the free and the bound are beyond the power games or manipulations that we can observe. There are "invisible loyalties" towards one's own family that follow rules, at times paradoxical, so that a child who is manifestly rebellious or delinquent, could be the person most loyal to his own family (Boszormenyi-Nagy and Spark, 1973).

> Carlo (Daniela's client) is a 47-year-old man who has always lived with his family in a state of subservience, incapable of maintaining work for any length of time. He shows many symptoms of depression and has had thirty years of unacknowledged psychophysical suffering.
> He tells me the story of his family: His father is a reasonably successful professional man, but very violent at home. His mother is a housewife who suffers from depressive episodes and is a suicide risk. Of his older brother he says: "he caused my parents all kinds of problems". In the family Carlo has taken the role of scapegoat, and when I inform him of this hypothesis, he breathes a sigh of relief, as if for the first time someone has understood his suffering, and so given his life recognition and dignity.

In these cases Hellinger speaks of unconscious dynamics such as: "I sacrifice myself for you", "I'll do it for you", or worse, "I'll die instead of you", with grave consequences for the life of the person who takes on the suffering of others, as in Carlo's case.

Hierarchical structure

The second Order of Love is:

Each one of us occupies a precise place within the family. There is a hierarchical order such that some occupy a higher place and come first, while others are inferior and come later (Hellinger, 2010a).

This hierarchical order between family members is given by their role and by a "hierarchy of time": those who come earlier have priority over those who come later. No connotation of value is attributed to this hierarchical order. It is neither good nor bad. What is subordinate being not less important because of it.

Every family and group system has a hierarchical order that derives from the members' held roles and from the time of their first belonging to it. The concept is clear when you refer to temporal order: parents are born before children, grandparents are born before their children and grandchildren, and so on. Even in business organizations you find a hierarchical order that depends on the members' function, role and the job they do, as well as on the temporal order.

Things get complicated when, in families and in organizations, the hierarchical order is not respected. For example, when a later arrival receives greater recognition than an earlier one, or worse, when someone assumes the right to take another's place.

For instance, in a family where the father is absent, if the mother, in her suffering, treats the eldest son as though he were her generational equal, the son might be flattered and seduced by this important role, but in the long run it can become a bond so heavy as to suffocate his life.

I (Daniela) recall many of my clients, men and women, who have had similar experiences in the family, and note how difficult it has been for them to have serious and satisfying emotional relationships outside the family.

Another example of "hierarchical overtaking" is when the kids feel they are so "big" as to intervene in the relationship between the parents.

> One of my (Daniela's) clients is the 25-year-old only daughter of a housewife and a banker. She has university studies to complete, but she is so angry with her parents that she spends more time railing against them than studying to gain her economic and emotional independence. She has always been a diligent and obedient daughter, close to her mother, indeed almost her shadow. But in the summer of 2013 she has an impossible love story, and it is then that the rift in the family begins, so much that the parents are alarmed and fear their beloved daughter has gone crazy. The girl asks me for support in trying to understand what is happening, whether she really is

going crazy, and in making her parents see that she wants to do other things in her life, not stay with them and endure their dynamics of dissatisfaction and perpetual tension.

When I ask her to describe her place in the family, she puts herself in between her father and mother.

This positioning is certainly legitimate and desirable for a child up to 8 or 10 years of age, but if, later, a person still sees herself there, it arouses the suspicion of some family disorder, an obstruction of growth and development in the person's life.

To place yourself between your parents when you are 25 may carry a sense of "keeper": "I stand here in between you, so I control you and stop you from separating or from hurting each other". In this case, to stand between the parents and evaluate them as a couple is an example of "hierarchical overtaking".

Another interesting example showing lack of respect for the hierarchical order is seen when, in a couple, greater importance is given to the children than to the partner. In our current reality this kind of disorder is common, and takes up considerable space in the various educational, health and therapeutic agencies.

So the parents have precedence over the children and the firstborn comes before the second.

THEORY

The flow of give and take from above to below and the flow of time from before to after cannot be stopped, nor reversed; it is not possible to change its direction, nor invert it from below to above and from after to before. Therefore, children are always below their parents, and those who come later always submit to those who come before. Give and take, and with them, time, flow always forwards, never backwards (Hellinger, 2008).

Parents' love for each other nourishes, heals and feeds the love for their children, not vice versa.

With a separation, the hierarchy of values changes, and if another partner comes on the scene,

The love for the children takes precedence over the love for the new partner. New partners often do not respect the precedence that is due to the children, and wish to take first place. That is not possible. It will only happen when they themselves have a child. If this order is not followed, an irremediable discord ensues (Ulsamer, 1999).

Another important factor of hierarchical order for the success of a couple relationship is to let go of the original family to build the new nuclear family.

In this regard Hellinger states:

The systems, too, have between them a hierarchical succession, which, however, is inverted. The new system takes

precedence over the old. For example, the current family has precedence over the family of origin (Hellinger, 1998).

For a relationship to work well, both partners should let go of their original family. All of us should be able to let go of the rules that obtained within our family of origin, and agree upon new ones that satisfy both members of the new family. In this way the new couple can have a satisfying intimate relationship. Some people say they are satisfied with the family they came from, but they do not get along with the partner's original family. This can poison a couple's relationship. When a person marries, he becomes part of his acquired family. This entails love and respect for the partner's family members, as well as for the partner. Only thus will the love be lasting (Ulsamer, 1999).

Also in the Organizational or Business Constellations, tied to the world of work, much attention is given to these different Orders. Unlike the Family Constellations, where emotional life is at times intense and deep, in the Organizational ones the focus is on the efficient functioning in and of the group, with the goal of solving specific work problems, enhancing professional success, and creating a good climate in the company.

In the Organizational Constellations I (Marco) have led, I have often identified problems of a familial nature transferred to the work environment. One of these is the difficulty in relating to authority, a problem which echoes, unconsciously, the relationship with a parent figure. Yet another problem is that of not feeling in the right place. One who does not find his place, did not feel right in his family, and will find it hard to feel right in his professional role. To feel in place, you should have received enough. It is from your proper place that you can give. Every movement towards others, success and life, or towards isolation, failure and death, faithfully traces the movement you have experienced towards your own parents.

In the world of work, unlike the family system, the hierarchy is established mainly by function. Nevertheless, what also counts is the temporal hierarchy in which, within the same function, those who arrive later are subordinate to those who arrived earlier. When all the professionals in the hierarchy feel in their right place, are motivated and responsible, work effectively, and support their subordinates, the system is in order. But this order is not in itself enough to guarantee success if the whole system, and all members with their functions, do not adopt a perspective of service to their customers (Hellinger, 2010b).

Balance between give and take

Life is sustained by the reciprocity between what one gives and what one receives during the generations, both in the vertical and horizontal sense. This holds for love and for everything good and useful that one can give and receive.

The right balance between giving and receiving among the people who belong to a family system, seems to be an implicit value, legitimate and justified, but, as we all know, it corresponds neither to the familial nor the personal reality.

How often have we heard said: "The sins of the father will be visited upon the children"? And how many times have we thought: "What has this to do with me?".

The grand ledger of giving and receiving has always been an essential concept of family ties.

> Nicola (Daniela's client) receives an unexpected inheritance from an elderly paternal aunt, a childless widow. He is young and needs money to start a small enterprise, so it seems a dream and he is happy about it.
> When he comes to my study, he looks worn out, thin, and doesn't smile. He has recently turned 35 but looks much older.
> "What's happening?" I ask him, and in a faint voice he tells me that all his problems started with the inheritance. He has had to tackle legal matters of which he was completely in the dark: an older brother of the aunt contested the will and was waging an aggressive legal battle. According to this brother, the

inheritance was due him, since he had looked after his sister when she was little, and had renounced his studies for her and for the family's wellbeing.

"What do you lose if you listen to this uncle?". Nicola thinks for a long while and at the next session tells me he has made an accurate investigation of the father's family. Indeed it happened as the uncle said, and Nicola's father, who is still alive, testified that the brother had for a long time provided for the family, and that after all the money was rightfully his.

The values of justice and loyalty that Nicola had acquired and shared with his parents led him to a reconciliation with his uncle. In doing so, Nicola does not know he has freed himself and his children from "generational debt".

Relationships between relatives and partners are based on principles of reciprocal loyalty and responsibility that allow and favor trust: these are the prerequisites for the health and wellbeing of relationships.

In the relationship between parents and children the give-and-have exchange has a different dynamic. Bringing a child into the world creates a particularly strong bond with both partner and child.

Becoming a parent implies an evolutionary passage in the personal, collective and spiritual consciousness: "Now that I am a parent, my point of view, my responsibilities and my priorities change."

The order of love between parents and children is defined first by the rule that parents give and children take. The parents give to the children what they have previously taken from their parents and what they take from each other as a couple. In the first place, the children accept their parents as parents; in the second place, they accept everything their parents give them. The children in turn transmit what they have received, especially to their future children. They can give because they have previously taken from their parents; and their children can take because in future they will give to their children (Hellinger, 2008).

This order of give and take also holds for brothers and sisters. Whoever arrives first must give to those who follow. Whoever follows must accept from those who were there before. This means the first child must give to the second and third; the second takes from the first and gives to the third, who in turn must take from the first and from the second. The oldest child gives the most and the youngest takes the most. In return, the youngest child often takes care of the elderly parents (Hellinger, 2008).

Parents give something to the children that the latter will never be able to return: they give life and take care of them as best they can. In the dynamic of the exchange, the children can help the parents if they need it in old age. Or they can give to their own children if they have any. Or they can compensate what they have received from their parents by helping others in voluntary or socially useful work.

The family is like a small company in which everyone should contribute. The parents can ask their children for collaboration, but if the parents' requests go beyond the children's possibilities, a perverse relationship ensues. If a parent seeks consolation from his children, if the children cannot defend themselves from such a demand, they become entangled in dynamics that will later prove punishing for them, such as causing their own failure or sabotaging their own goals.

How can a person come out of such disorders? "There is only one way to leave: to understand the order and accept it with love. Understanding the order is wisdom, and submitting to it with love is humility" (Hellinger, 2008).

In my work as school counselor, I (Daniela) often, and increasingly, should face and listen to separated parents who lay many expectations on their kids, as compensation for their own emotional failures.

My position, when I meet these parents – who are often angry and desperate – has changed over time, and thanks to my systemic-relational training and experience with Family Constellations, I have resolutely practiced this understanding and have come out of the linear model of cause and blame, preferring to observe the "Orders of Love".

Orders of Love and of Helping

Recently a woman asked me for help with her kids because her partner had left about a year ago, had ended their relationship and, what made her even angrier, is no longer in touch with the daughters. Her request to me was: "Please tell me how I can call him back to his duties as father". I looked at her calmly and quite seriously said: "You can't".

Thus I invite parents to declare their intentions and to look benevolently at their own responsibilities, towards themselves, their ex-partner, and their kids. This kind of conversation is most effective in creating order in relationships.

The relationship between equals, such as that between couples and groups of friends, deserves special reflection.

In the couple, love alone is not enough. For it to work, the couple must let go of power struggles, arguing over who is right and who is wrong, offence and disappointment. But most of all, as Hellinger observes, it is necessary to acknowledge the Orders needed for the love to flow and to evolve.

A basic premise for a good relationship of the couple is that there be balance between give and take.

Happiness in a relationship depends on the free exchange between give and take. A meagre exchange will bring poor returns. The greater the exchange: the deeper the happiness.

However this has a big disadvantage: it is more binding. Those who want their own freedom must give and take in small quantities, and surrender only in a limited fashion.

You can give only as much as you are able to give, and only when the other is ready to receive. If you give more than the other is ready to receive, the partner will feel oppressed, will be even less disposed to give, and the imbalance will keep increasing (Ulsamer, 1999).

Orders of Helping

Just as there are certain systemic laws governing families and groups, so there are laws for therapists and in general for all the helping professions that try to render a service to their clients: The Orders of Helping (Hellinger, 2006). These orders were discovered by Hellinger during many years' experience with the Family Constellations.

As a psychotherapist, Hellinger observed for many years the nature of the relationship between therapist and client, and what it was that made therapy a success or failure.

What happens in the therapeutic encounter? The client turns to the therapist for help and this places the therapist in a position of superiority in relation to the client in need. Furthermore, the therapist temporarily enters into the life of the client, thus also taking a place in her family system.

Hellinger observes that in many traditional therapies, above all the psychodynamic approach, what is established is a relation he ironically calls a "therapeutic rapport", in other words, the therapist substitutes some figure of the client's family system (transference and countertransference).

When in traditional therapy someone turns to a therapist for help, what happens in that moment? A transference arises from the child to the parents and a countertransference arises from the therapist to the client, as from the father and mother to the child. Inevitably a long therapy ensues, destined to fail, unless the client decides to get angry with the therapist and end the therapy. Anyhow, few manage to do this (Hellinger, 2006).

According to Hellinger, when a therapist takes such a position, he weakens the client and generates an entanglement which makes him unable to take into consideration the whole family system, and in particular the excluded members. Moreover, the therapist's exclusive empathy or sympathy towards the client causes him inwardly to judge other members of the system, and thus to collude with the very problem that the client brings to therapy, thus contributing to its maintenance instead of solving it. It will therefore mean a disorder that prevents the therapist from efficaciously helping the client, and will make the therapist prolong the therapy beyond a reasonable time limit without achieving success.

In order for help or therapy to be successful, it must respect certain orders that make the client and her family system stronger, whole, and free. For this to be possible, the helper must encourage responsibility, reconciliation and autonomy, showing humility and respect.

The first order of help consists in giving only what you have and in expecting and accepting only what you need.
The first disorder of help begins when you want to give what you don't have, and take what you don't need (Hellinger, 2006).

Giving and taking have their limits, and to acknowledge this, facilitates growth. The therapist must know what he can and cannot give the client, that is, what he can and cannot do for her, and must establish it and agree with her about it from the start. This clarity helps the therapist set himself limits, and set limits for the unrealistic or childish expectations the client may have. Furthermore, it ensures that what is the client's, remains hers: for example her responsibility and her destiny.

As a good teacher does not replace the student in the student's exams, so that in facing and handling them she will become stronger and abler, so a helper must leave to the other and to her system of belonging their tasks, responsibilities, and above all their destiny. Otherwise a helper replaces a figure greater than the client, such as a mother, father or even God, and in so doing, keeps her in an infantile position and participates in that family's destinies.

How is all this translated into practice? In the first session the therapist establishes with the client whether he can help her, or whether it is better for the client to go to other professionals. The therapist who works with Family Constellations should explain to the client that his approach includes attention to the whole family system, not merely to the individual, and that it aims at the essential without going further. If the therapist can help the client, he establishes with her a "therapeutic contract" in which are defined the goals, times, and ways of reaching these goals, and what will show both that they have been reached.

This framework sets the boundaries of the professional intervention, helps the therapist direct his work and the client to define and to expect what she needs. Based on this agreement and reciprocal trust a therapeutic alliance is created: a collaboration.

Considering the first order of help, approximately how long should a therapeutic intervention take? Hellinger believes it should end as soon as change in the right direction is activated, in other words, the moment the client gets more strength. This is apparent when the movement leading to the solution arises. This is sufficient because it is the manifestation of what is essential, which is in harmony with the soul and therefore effective. Usually this happens when the client succeeds in looking at the excluded ones, victims and perpetrators, and in feeling empathy for them; when she takes responsibility for what has happened, or in any case manages to accept and face the situation, her own life and her destiny as it is. In any case it occurs with a movement that reunifies what was previously divided.

> *Thus begins a movement of the soul that allows us to unite what was previously divided. As soon as the movement arises, I interrupt the representation. There is no reason to continue to be involved. When the soul has gained command, the facilitator is superfluous.*
> *This is the best way to help. We do not seek a decisive solution. When this is set in motion, we can leave the client to her soul (Hellinger, 2006).*

These days a counseling intervention takes one to five weekly, fortnightly or monthly sessions. The short-term psychotherapies take about ten weekly sessions. The short-term systemic-family therapies consist of about ten fortnightly or monthly sessions, the longer ones of twenty sessions, also fortnightly or monthly (Boscolo and Bertrando, 1996). With the Family Constellations we have found it possible to bring about change in a single session.

Assagioli, the founder of Psychosynthesis, profoundly believed in the principle of responsibility, and already in the 1960's held that a psychotherapeutic or counseling intervention should be as brief as possible, so as not to encourage dependency (Moretti, 2010).

The more numerous and closer together are the sessions, the greater is the likelihood of creating what Hellinger calls a "therapeutic rapport", one based on transference and countertransference. Nevertheless, if the therapist does not assume the appropriate attitude and position towards the client and her family system, he may undermine the first order of help even at the first encounter. This means that for the help to have any force, it must be as brief as possible and as effective as necessary.

What is the price paid by a therapist who subverts the first order of help? The lesser price is encouraging the transference of the client, who will behave more and more childishly towards him. The medium price is that the therapist and client cannot grow, and become weak instead of gaining strength and freedom. The highest price is that they enter a shared destiny, in other words, that the destiny of the client and her family becomes the destiny of the therapist and his family, with all that this implies.

THEORY

The second order of helping therefore consists in submitting to the circumstances and intervening only to the extent that they allow. This help is fair, and has strength.
Here the disorder of helping consists in denying the circumstances instead of looking squarely at them with the person who needs help (Hellinger, 2006).

In my experience (Marco) with the Family Constellations I have often found myself helping clients with grave personal and familial pathologies. The work with the Constellations is work with destiny, with life and death. Only after having faced and embraced completely his own hurts and his own destiny, can the therapist help clients to the same. To accept life, death and destiny as they present themselves is what gives strength, freedom and serenity.

A big part of destiny is preordained: the soul has a history and enters a family with a story already written, the family is inserted into a context, a nation and a race, all of which in turn have a written history. Anything new the individual can write, therefore, does not depend solely on her but takes its strength and freedom from the respect of all that came before.

At the start of my career (Marco), like many of my colleagues, I made the mistake of helping others try to change their destiny. At the end of the day I was always exhausted. So I began to ask myself the reasons for that tiredness, and after a few months, thanks to supervision, I saw that something was amiss in my attitude. I realized that I ought not take away from clients their part of the responsibility, and I had to respect their destiny just as it was. Since then my attitude has changed and I have not felt tired since. At the end of a day's work, or even after demanding workshops, I feel fresh and light. My way of working is more effective too, because I have learned to be humble towards, and to accept, the circumstances and difficulties my clients bring me. I am thus able to perceive with greater clarity what essential and permitted intervention I need to make. I can look squarely at life and death, accept and welcome destiny as it is, and invite my clients to do the same. And when the movement of the soul has run its course, I take a step back and retire.

In the third order of helping the facilitator stands as an adult before an adult in search of help. In this way he foils the latter's attempts at relegating him to the role of parent [...].
The disorder of helping consists in allowing an adult to make demands of the facilitator like those of a son or daughter towards the parents, and occurs too when the facilitator treats the client as a child and rescues her from something that she can and must endure on her own (Hellinger, 2006).

As we have seen, the risk in all the helping professions is that the clients and therapists relate as if they were children and parents. In one sense it is inevitable that the client, in turning to someone for help, arouses in herself the parent-child relationship. The very fact of acknowledging ourselves in need, evokes in all of us the primordial image of help represented by the relationship of the mother to her child. The therapist wishing to establish an adult relation with his client must keep this in mind and act accordingly.

A client can succeed in her attempt to manipulate if the therapist also has a manipulative attitude. In other words, clients can manifest their transference only with therapists who try to satisfy their own needs in the therapeutic relationship (Nanetti, 2014).

An authentic therapist seeks an alliance, a collaboration with the adult part of the client, with whom he sets the goals, times and methods of intervention. When the child part of the client emerges, he receives it, but he also helps it to grow and assume responsibility, he gives it limits and avoids giving it sympathy. This attitude disappoints the client's childish expectations to give strength to her adult part. To the extent to which the client presents an infantile attitude towards the therapist, such disappointment may arouse frustration and anger in her. But this is positive for both because each is respected as an adult. It is then up to the therapist to receive and manage the client's frustration and anger within the treatment plan.

For example, if a client, complaining about an uncomfortable condition, assume an attitude that tries to move the therapist, and the therapist responds by leading the session with an attitude of sympathy, it will end up establishing a therapeutic relationship based on transference and countertransference. If instead the therapist listens and shows bodily empathy, helps the client to explore and deepen the emotions related to the problem, and finally, responds to her adult part, saying: "what could you do to resolve this problem?", the client feels supported and becomes responsible. She can now give space to her adult part, or she could further pursue the therapist in a self-pitying way, seeking sympathy, reassurance and advice, or again she could take an antagonistic position. It is right for the therapist to understand and help the client, but according to Hellinger, it is wrong if in doing so he fosters an infantile and manipulative attitude and creates a parent-child relationship.

In this regard Virginia Satir states:

Yet perhaps much of the patient's so-called transference was really an appropriate reaction to the therapist's behavior [...].
In addition, there was a greater change that the therapeutic situation would perpetuate pathology, instead of presenting a new state of affairs which would introduce doubts about the old perceptions (Satir, 1967).

The therapist's inner attitude that promotes the client's progress is to relate in an empathic, authentic way and bear in mind his relationship to his own and his client's parents. In other words, if the therapist behaves in an understanding, consistent way and visualizes the client's parents behind her, he respects them and inwardly bows to them; in relating to the client, he does not replace one of them.

> *To be successful, help must be systemic. Therefore, besides keeping in mind the client, you need to keep in mind her system too. Traditional psychotherapy is based on the relationship between client and therapist. If the therapist or facilitator sees the parents and ancestors behind the client, he receives them in his heart and inwardly bows to and respects their destiny, and if he feels behind himself his own destiny, his parents and ancestors, he is no longer alone, and it is no longer possible to establish a therapeutic rapport in the traditional sense of the term. A relationship is created between adults seeking a solution and acting in that direction (Hellinger, 2006).*

The therapist who does not consider his place and that of the client's family members, will tend to replace some person of the family system. In doing so, the therapist does not respect his place nor that of the client's parents, which means that inwardly he considers himself better than them. This disorder probably reflects an analogous disorder within the therapist's family, where he held a parental role in relation to his mother or father. In this case, before being able to help and heal others, he needs to heal himself by repositioning himself in his own family system.

The only case in which the therapist is justified in behaving like a parent towards the client is when, in doing the Constellations work, he represents one of them. It is in exceptional cases that the therapist deliberately and temporarily becomes the representative of the client's mother or father. It can happen that in individual or group therapy the client manifests the suffering of an interrupted movement towards the beloved person (see figure 2). The therapist can then represent a maternal or paternal figure and receive the client as the child of that time, to complete the embrace she needed. This is a representation, not a substitution. Finally, after this therapeutic action, he may withdraw from the representation and continue to visualize the client in the arms of her parents. In such cases, it is useful to declare that it is Family Constellation in which the therapist is not replacing, but simply representing, one of the parents.

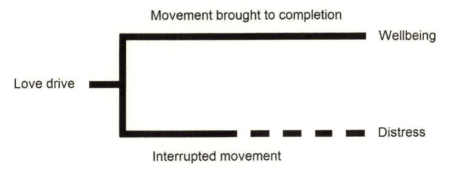

Figure 2

The interruption of the spontaneous loving movement towards the beloved causes emotional and physical pathologies: distress and psychosomatic disorders.

Unexpressed love can change into anger, grief, despair, resignation, and so on, accumulating in the body in the form of muscular contraction, pain and a sense of oppression. Furthermore, anyone who has experienced an interrupted movement of love at a tender age, relives it as an adult in relation to her partner: the experience of interruption is repeated in the body and the subject inhibits the movement of love in a way like how she experienced it in childhood (Hellinger, 1998).

In individual work there are various psycho-bodily techniques to help the client complete an interrupted movement (Liss and Stupiggia, 2000; Giommi and Cristofori, 2009; De Sario and Fiumara, 2015). Essentially,

> *The action that expresses emotions can eliminate the distress caused by the inhibition of the action, and can restore the capacity for spontaneous movement (Boadella and Liss, 1986).*

It creates a context in which the client can relive the moment of interruption, with all its pain and anger, and help her complete it so love can flow once again (Hellinger, 2008).

The bodily empathy, the therapist's tuning with the client (through mirroring posture, look, facial expressions, head movements, gestures, tone of voice, rhythm, intensity, breathing, and so on), encourages the client's psychophysical expression and contributes to making explicit what was previously implicit. Then, through certain psycho-bodily techniques that connect the body, sensations, breath, voice, emotional experience, mental images, thoughts, and movement, he helps the client to complete the process of disinhibiting the action, which repairs this inner relational "tear". When the therapist uses these techniques, he does so without replacing people of the client's family system. While working with her individually, he keeps in mind the relations implicated in the inhibition of the action, and in so doing, helps the client to restore that psychophysical and interpersonal process, that movement, which in her life had been interrupted.

> *So the facilitator must empathize not so much in a personal as in a systemic way. He must not establish a personal relationship with the client. This is the fourth order of helping. Here the disorder of help consists in not bearing in mind and not respecting other important people who hold the key to the solution, in particular the excluded members [...] (Hellinger, 2006).*

THEORY

The therapist establishes with the client a human and professional relationship based on a request for help that considers all the members of the client's family system, especially the excluded ones. The therapist's empathy is inclusive, not exclusive. His focus is the client's whole system, not just the client. Therefore Hellinger says that the therapist must not establish a personal relationship. The work with the Family Constellations, though requested by the individual, is systemic work.

One of the big limitations of non-systemic psychotherapy and counseling is the fact of working exclusively with the individual: such interventions are effective to the extent that the psychological disorders and wounds have an entirely personal history.

Often we suffer from problems that are not the result of unprocessed events that happened to us, but rather are the consequence of traumas suffered by other people in our system. We are joined for generations to the communal destinies of the family and the lineage, to the effects of the traumas that concern a whole system of relations, and to the "orders of love" that without our knowing or wanting, entangle us in the destiny of others (Schneider and Schneider, 2006).

Mariangela (a client of Marco) is a 25-year-old girl in therapy to resolve her phobia of lifts. Every time she enters a lift she has a panic attack. In the first session I explore her problem, how her discomfort manifests, and all the associated emotions. I also ask her for information about her family of origin.

At the second session Mariangela relates a dream in which she is stuck in a lift with another woman. The lift keeps going down... she feels as if her head will explode... and she wakes up with a start, gripped by unbearable anguish. It is an important dream that gives me precious systemic information, but I decide not to go into it for the moment. Instead I ask Mariangela to talk to me about her family. She tells me she left a few years ago to make her own life. She also says she is very worried about her parents and angry with her father. I ask her to write a letter to her father, a letter she will not send, so she can feel free to write what she wants to him.

Mariangela brings the letter to the third meeting, tells me what she felt in writing it, and about the anger towards her father for having neglected her mother. In her description I get the feeling that Mariangela has taken on states of mind that are not hers. I suggest this idea to her and ask her to re-read the letter to herself to understand how much of the anger is hers and how much is her mother's. After re-reading it Mariangela tells me half the anger is not hers, but her mother's. I propose an Individual Constellation. I ask her to close her eyes, visualize her mother, and sense in her body where she feels the part of the anger that isn't hers. She feels it in her throat. I ask her to put her hands on her throat, perceive the anger, and, if she feels it, to give it back to her mother. After doing this, Mariangela starts crying and feels pain in her belly. So I ask her to put her hands on her belly and get in touch with the pain. I then ask her how much of that pain is hers. She tells me it is not hers, but her mother's. I ask her to give this too back to her, if she feels like it. She agrees, and suddenly, straight afterwards, she remembers that before being conceived, her mother had had an abortion. I ask her to visualize her mother with this baby: the baby screams and cries because the mother doesn't want it, so Mariangela takes it in her arms. I ask her to look at her mother and tells her: "Till now I have done this for you. But it is your child and up to you to take care of it". Mariangela speaks this sentence to her mother, who takes the baby in her arms and sighs with relief. I ask Mariangela to ask the baby its name. The baby smiles at her and says it is Giuseppe. I then ask Mariangela to visualize her father next to her mother and tell them: "Dear mother and father, what happened between you two is not my responsibility: it is yours and I give it back to you". And then to turn to her brother: "Dear Giuseppe, I am your sister and this is your mum and your dad. You will always have a place in our heart and our family". Mariangela is very moved and visibly relieved. Now the meaning of the dream is quite clear to me, so as she is leaving my studio, I say: "Taking the lift will now be easier". When she arrives for the next session Mariangela is radiant: she could take the lift without any fear.

The systemic work begins in one's soul. This means I must not look only at the client, but also at her family. If it finds a place in my heart, I am in perfect harmony and gain the strength to do what is needed. And no transference occurs. This is the revolutionary aspect of the method (Hellinger, 2006).

Orders of Love and of Helping

When the therapist looks in this way at the client's whole system, he has the capacity to perceive what is essential. In other words, the Knowing Field can guide the therapist so that his attention and empathy are catalyzed by the excluded members of the family. The role of the therapist, then, is also that of helping the client to look and feel empathy for the excluded ones. If also the client's attention and empathy shift onto excluded members of her family, the healing movement of the soul occurs: the movement of reunification. The therapist therefore has the role of facilitating this movement of the soul and then withdrawing. This is the reason Hellinger calls the therapist who works with Family Constellations "facilitator".

> *The fifth order of helping is thus love towards all, as they are, however different from us they may be. In this way the facilitator opens his heart. He becomes part of the other. What is reconciled in his heart, is reconciled in the client's system too.*
>
> *Here the disorder of help is judgment of others, usually a condemnation, tied to moral indignation. One who truly helps, does not judge (Hellinger, 2006).*

Often the excluded members of the family are aborted and forgotten babies, the victims and perpetrators of the past, prostitutes, the mentally ill and in general all those who have meant shame for the family. All those who have been excluded and their personal characteristics thus go to make up the "family's shadow". The more a member is excluded, the more his personal characteristics become autonomous through the shadow, executing a possessive action on the family. In this way the shadow takes on all the unacceptable tendencies, characteristics and attitudes. And the more the shadow is repressed, the more it is forced to react and take on hostile elements.

The collective consciousness tends to exclude all that has caused a significant wound, scandal or shame within the family. But in doing so, just as in Archimedes' principle, it creates a splitting movement that tends to be offset by an opposite movement, so that other members of the family will have to impersonate the ones who have been excluded.

When the client goes to the therapist, in a certain sense she is entangled like her whole family in the movement of exclusion and compensation just described. If the therapist relates in an exclusive and personal way with the client, he too becomes entangled in this movement of exclusion. If instead the therapist relates empathically to the client's whole family system, he can be guided by the Knowing Field and efficaciously help her and her system of belonging.

The Spiritual Consciousness, unlike the collective one, works to hook up what was previously splitted, starting from the relationship with the parents, and up to all the excluded members, including all the victims and perpetrators of the past. The therapist facilitates healing when he places himself in tune with the Spiritual Consciousness: when he abstains from judging, opens his heart and puts himself in touch with the soul and the Spiritual Consciousness, where healing originates. Then he can include in himself all those who have been excluded from the client's family system. Finally, this movement, which starts from the therapist's soul, can be translated into the movement of the client's soul.

The Family Constellations operate in the service of the Spiritual Consciousness and of reconciliation. For that to be possible, the therapist must first carry out on himself the work of contact and connection with the soul and the Love of the Spirit. He must do the work of reunification within his own family system. He will thus be able to work, beyond the concepts of good and evil, in the service of the Spiritual Consciousness, giving a place in his own soul to all the members of the client's family, and especially to the excluded ones. This is the revolutionary aspect of the Family Constellations.

Individual Systemic Interview
by Marco Moretti and Daniela Poggioli

I (Daniela) am specialized in Systemic-Relational Therapy and have spent many years combining the systemic concepts I acquired in my academic training with the hundreds of systemic experiences I have observed in families during Family Constellations workshops.

Prior to this my therapeutic systemic-relational work (like that of many colleagues) was based on the interview with the family, the couple, or the individual, so it was mainly a verbal approach.

The circular interview, the reflexive or hypothetical questions, that we carried out in our therapeutic settings with a systemic-relational approach, had good results in the therapies and undoubtedly helped many families, couples, and persons open to new experiences and other possible ways of dealing with psychological and relational suffering.

When you work with the group Family Constellations, all this disappears and you witness, or participate in, emotionally involving scenes, where the relational dynamics take place before the incredulous eyes of the client and audience present. Here we enter the sphere of phenomenological philosophy, where things happen and are not told.

THEORY

The individual counseling and therapy sessions, compared to the group workshops in Family Constellations, make more use of verbal narration. The client turns to the therapist with the expectation of being listened to, to tell her story, and this desire must be usefully and constructively received, from both the human and the therapeutic point of view.

For us, systemic therapy [with individuals] now means to enter with the client into a complex network of ideas, emotions, and significant persons, recursively connected and explored by the two interlocutors through language (Boscolo and Bertrando, 1996).

These days various manuals exist on empathic listening, counseling, and the clinical interview. A good therapist should have a thorough knowledge of this theoretical material, and have acquired it through adequate training and professional supervision.

In individual counseling and therapy, when we (Marco and Daniela) work with the Individual Family Constellations, we combine the therapeutic use of the word as clinical interview, and the techniques of representation with dolls (Daniela), sheets of paper, free space and visualizations (Marco), each within his or her specific work methodology.

Given that in individual work with the Family Constellations it is crucial to consider the individual as integral part of her family system, we find it useful to mention a few principles that characterize individual systemic counseling and psychotherapy (Boscolo and Bertrando, 1996; Hellinger, 2006; Edelstein, 2007; Tramonti and Fanali, 2013).

In the individual session the therapist and the client are facing each other in a relationship of reciprocal collaboration, responsibility and "influence", in which the client's family system meets the therapist's family system. Both figures, in fact, in the therapeutic encounter, are bearers of all their relationships. Furthermore, given that the therapist and the client are meeting because of a request for help, the therapist temporarily enters into the client's family system. According to the orders of helping identified by Hellinger (2006), the therapist is regarded as the latest arrival with respect to all the components of the client's family system. The therapist must therefore bear in mind, right to the end of the therapeutic relationship, that he occupies the last place in the client's system.

To foster this attitude of "systemic awareness", it is useful for the therapist to imagine that in his studio, together with the client in flesh and bone, are other different components of his current and original family, at her side and behind her, respectively. This is "an imaginative evocation". This kind of visualization helps the therapist be aware, when working individually with the client, that while he is relating to her, at the same time he is relating to the rest of her family too. This visualization, moreover, helps the therapist develop an inclusive, systemic empathy, not focused solely on the client.

> *It is a systemic empathy. As a facilitator, I do not look only at the client the moment she says something or expects empathy from me. I look at her family. In this way I am aware of who really needs my empathy. Often the client is the one who needs it the least. On the contrary, I must relate to her so that she shows empathy for others, instead of expecting it from me (Hellinger, 2006).*

Working with systemic criteria also has other bases and guidelines (Boscolo and Bertrando, 1996):

1. To think about making hypotheses rather than diagnoses. This is a true revolution in academic thinking because diagnosis had dominated psychiatry and psychoanalytic therapy from their origin to the present day. Hypothesis has the function of connecting data obtained from listening to and observing the client. It is neither true nor false, only more or less useful. Hypothesis is still a good tool in conducting a session, since it allows the therapist to connect information, meanings, and actions that emerge in the dialogue, while always considering the time and context in which the family or

individual lives. It is important to verify the plausibility of the hypotheses and change them when necessary in the course of time.
2. To evaluate the plausibility of the hypotheses, the therapist uses the principle of circularity, that is, the capacity to lead his investigation by basing himself on the client's feedback, verbal and nonverbal, to the information about the relationships and differences between herself and the members of the family.
3. To think about the other, the client, with curiosity and understanding.

The systemic therapist's thinking is based on the complementarity of linear and circular concepts of causality, on the plurality of viewpoints, and on a preference for asking questions rather than giving answers; and all this has the effect, over time, of conveying to the client a way of connecting things and people, events and meanings, that will free her from the rigid view of herself and the reality that surrounds her. In this way the client frees herself of a story that has become cumbersome and a source of suffering, and is able to create a new story that offers greater freedom and autonomy (Boscolo and Bertrando, 1996).

Although the therapist's theoretic approach may be neither instructive nor normative, he nevertheless belongs to a culture and thus cannot but have his own ideology about what "right", or "wrong", "appropriate" or not appropriate", "healthy" or "sick". Such an ideology must be consciously set apart so it does not interfere with client solution attempts.

Another way of describing the therapeutic process is to say the therapist, through his "circular questions", encourages reflections and thoughts so the client can conceive a new representation of her reality and a re-reading of her experiences. Thanks to this reorganization of her own experience, the client can again see her and others' position within the meaningful system of which she is part.

The aim of the circular questions is to interconnect the relations, ideas, emotions and behaviors that are manifest in the client's relationships.

> *[...] The information obtained through circular questioning is reciprocal: through questions, both clients and therapists constantly change their understanding on the basis of the information offered by others. Circular questions bring news about differences, new connections between ideas, meanings, and behaviour (Boscolo and Bertrando, 1996).*

Some kinds of circular questions are (Selvini Palazzoli *et al.*, 1980):

- Triadic questions, in which you ask a person to comment on the relationship between two others members of the family. For example: "What does your son do when his father criticizes you?".

- Questions on differences in behavior between two or more people, instead of on intrinsic qualities of the person. For example: "When you are sad, how do your husband and children behave?".
- Questions about changes in behavior before or after a specific event. For example: "Did your daughter stop eating before or after her grandmother's death?".
- Questions about hypothetical circumstances. For example: "What would you two parents do if your son were to go and live on his own?".
- Classifications of family members according to a specific behavior or interaction. For example: "Which of your family members is most able to support you in difficult moments?".

The art of conducting a therapeutic dialogue consists also in the capacity to suggest to the client plausible hypotheses, which, through the circular questions, construct new meanings.

Giovanna (a client of Daniela) is a 50-year-old woman, married and with a 20-year-old daughter (Paola), who is enrolled at University and soon to move to another town. Giovanna arrives with far more anxiety than warranted by the situation she describes to me, and after an investigation of the nuclear family and her family of origin, I suggest to her that she describe more fully this anxiety and tell me when it started to increase.

G: "Look, I have always been an anxious type, but now I feel I'm going crazy and am so worried about my daughter that at every moment I feel like I'm suffocating."

T: "But if Paola were here, what would she say?".

G: "Oh she would say I shouldn't worry, she'll be just fine, and if she needs anything she will call us, and she really wants to have this experience."

T: "Here I feel like asking "who is protecting whom?"".

G: "Hmm!" (she smiles)! I don't know, maybe I'm exaggerating, but it's as if with her going away I felt very weak."

The conversation proceeds and at the end of the meeting I suggest a different implication to her "worry and feeling of suffocation".

T: "It really seems that your daughter is giving you an important opportunity for you to lessen your role of mother and let grow the wishes that have been buried in some remote place! What do you think?".

G: (She keeps her head down a while and thinks). "You know, what you say lifts my spirits a bit. We have been dealing with our daughter's problems for so long that I have forgotten about myself to a degree, like I did with my parents… and let me tell you I often dream of being pregnant… what would that mean?".

T: "What comes to your mind?".

G: "Well… seeing as I am in menopause, I don't think it has to do with another child. It occurs to me that a friend of mine always had this dream, and one day she said these dreams were the manifestation of unfulfilled wishes…".

T: "Interesting, don't you think?".

All this brings up the question of responsibility, both that of the client, who makes choices and distinctions in interpreting her world, and of the therapist, who, through his competence, must help the client enlarge her interpretative framework, without trying to guide her in a parental kind of relationship (Tramonti and Fanali, 2013).

The circular questions, like any other conversational technique, do not directly change the client's point of view, but activate new reflections that may enhance other thoughts, other connections, and consequently develop new relational dynamics.

A young client of mine (Daniela), a university student, was convinced her parents wanted her to return home and that her studies would not open the way to a good job. Her conviction grew stronger the more depressed her mother was. During the sessions and our investigations into the relational modes shown by various members of the family, including aunts, uncles and grandparents, she realized that her belief was tied to her fear of disappointing everyone, more particularly that she was the first in the family to undertake such a tough course of study, and that: "Many envy this capacity of mine and some have said they were proud of me and that I at last represent the "new" in a very modest family...".

THEORY

Thanks to circular questions it is possible, moreover, to *evoke* in the therapeutic setting the presence/absence of family figures through a "narrative evocation".

> *[The systemic family therapist] in this way [...] works on a series of triadic or polyadic relationships, rather than on the dyad that comes about with a single client.*
>
> *Such a position left its mark on individual systemic therapy. It may be expressed through the introduction, within the dual relationships between therapist and client, of voices, presence, points of view – briefly of the words of the third parties that are relevant to the life of a client. The systemic therapist is strongly interested in the way her client sees others. Initially, this interest was put into practice by evoking the significant third parties in the life of the client, mainly through circular questions, summoning their presence on to the scene of the therapy. Boscolo and Bertrando [1996] have called this procedure "presentification of the third party" (Bertrando, 2002).*

Presentification or evoking the third party can be done in at least two ways:

1. It can happen through questions that introduce into the dialogue people who are important to the client, for example: "What opinion would your mother express on what you are saying?". "How would your father feel about

what you have just told me?", and so on. Such questions can include voices, personality traits, and even bodily parts of the client: "How does your stomach feel when you tell me this event?". "What does your inner child still expect from your mother?", and so on.

2. Sometimes you ask the client to picture, seated on the chair next to her, the presence of a family member, or a part of herself, and to establish a real dialogue. This can be regarded as a true preamble to the techniques of the Individual Constellations, and allows you to see how ready the client is to undertake one.

Elisa (a client of Daniela) is a 25-year-old who is feeling blocked in her university studies. She asks for therapeutic help to overcome this predicament and to attain economic independence, though she does not have any prospects in the short term. She is very angry with her parents because they criticize her and urge her to finish her studies. Here I give a short example showing the function of circular questions.

T: "So you're saying your parents don't understand what you are doing".
Elisa: "Yes, and I think they don't approve of what I'm doing".
T: "What do you think they don't approve of?".
E: "The fact that I devote myself to many things but not to my studies".
T: "What do you think?".

E: "I think they are too accustomed to their world and don't relate to the new world of young people, and that things are different nowadays to how they experienced them."
T: "What would your father say if he were here?".
E: "In what sense?".
T: "What would your father say if he were sitting on that chair?".
E: "He'd say these things are a waste of time; they don't amount to anything."
T: "What in your opinion makes him think that?".
E: "Well... the fact that at my age he and my mother already had a job...".
T: "And what else?".
E: "Well... I think he is worried about me, and so is my mother, but she in a different way: she listens to me more."
T: "So if they were here both would say these things?".
E: "Actually, yes... well, I understand them a bit!".

The conversation proceeds; I invite Elisa to go into the various points of view, to reflect on the rigidity of her interpretations, and to form ideas that are less stereotypical. In this way she can broaden and deepen her own sensitivity, and discover the events and stories that concern her in a multiple perspective, instead of in the learned perspective, which causes her to relate to herself and other family members in a rigid and repetitive way.

Another way of "evoking the third party" is the "intuitive evocation". In conversation with the client, the therapist may experience physical sensations, emotions, states of mind; or mental images may arise. In the psychodynamic therapies these phenomena come under the category of transference and countertransference (Gill, 1982). In the Family Constellations, however, we know that in the dyadic relationship with the client, the Knowing Field acts too, and informs – more often the therapist than the client – about what needs to be integrated. The therapist should discern whether this information, in the form of sensations, emotions, states of mind and mental images, concerns only him or also the client, and, in the latter case, should at the right moment feed them back as hypotheses through circular questions.

> Igina (client of Marco) is an approximately 40-year-old woman, who ardently desires a child. At our first meeting she expresses this wish and tells me about her difficulties in the relationship with her partner. She cries a lot and complains about the failure of their attempts at conceiving a child. As I listen empathically, an image of a thirty-year-old young woman arises in my mind. I have a daughter about that age, so I think this image may concern me. Anyhow I decide to keep her in mind. I ask my client to say something more about her life, and she tells me she is divorced. As the image of the young woman comes back into my mind, I ask Igina: "What would your previous partner think of the fact that you so want a child?".

THEORY

She is momentarily dumbfounded, and says she already has a twenty-nine-year-old daughter with her ex-husband.

As in the group Family Constellations, a representative is never chosen "by chance", and often has considerable affinities with the person represented; thus I, like Igina, have a daughter that age. The Knowing Field presented the image of the person who was excluded, at least from the client's narration, and who was asking to be included again. Since it was the first session, and we did not yet have a therapeutic alliance, I didn't ask a direct question to find out if she had other children: instead I decided to "making-present" her ex-husband, as she herself had mentioned him. With a circular question the focus widened to other relationships, and during following sessions Igina understood that her pain was not only due to not being able to have another child: above all it referred to the fact of not having succeeded in building a good relationship with her daughter, to whom she had given birth at sixteen, and who was raised by the grandparents. At the end of the counseling Igina decided to reconstruct and improve the relationship with her daughter.

Ornella (client of Marco) seeks counseling to settle a few family disagreements. In the second session she tells me a detailed dream in which are present several people Ornella does not recognize, one of whom is trying repeatedly to enter her home. During the narration of the dream I experience a sense of anguish. While I am feeling this state of mind, Ornella instead smiles. At the end of her narration I decide to making-present the anguish through a circular question: "In your opinion who would be anguished in a situation such as that of the dream?" Ornella stays silent for a bit and then talks to me about her mother, whom she has not seen for a long while and with whom she wants nothing more to do.

Thus the Knowing Field acts as a source of information that allows unconscious contents and excluded members of the system to be reintegrated, with all their sensations, emotions and states of mind, towards a greater systemic harmony.

Luisella (client of Marco), at our fifth session, describes to me a conflict she had with her mother the day before. The conflict arose because Luisella realized she had replaced her mother in the management of her younger brother. During her narration I feel cold shivers. This sensation is usually associated with unresolved grief. So, when Luisella has finished talking, I ask: "Whom has your mother lost?". Luisella thinks for a moment and answers that her mother hasn't lost anybody. I then ask her if her mother has ever had an abortion. Luisella is amazed and tells me that indeed her mother, in between her and her younger brother, had an abortion.
An image comes to my mind of her mother crouched beside this baby. So I say to Luisella: "I picture your mother crouched on the ground beside this dead child. You are standing and holding

in your arms your new-born brother. Your mother says to you: "You take care of him in my place", and you reply: "I will do it for you". Luisella starts to cry and in between sobs says: "That's exactly how it went". I give her all the time she needs to express her pain, and then add: "Now your brother is grown up and has a family of his own. So you can look at your mother and tell her: "There, I did it for you. Now I can live my life". At these words Luisella takes a deep breath and cheers up: the anger at her mother has gone. Now she feels able to invest in her own future.

The physical sensations, emotions, states of mind and mental images that the therapist experiences in the encounter with a client can arise for at least five reasons:

1. Interactive resonances and responses that happen in all human relationships.
2. Resonances and responses triggered by the client and reinforced by the personal problems of the therapist (interlocking interaction).
3. Transference of the therapist towards the client. That is, the therapist relates to the client as if she were a significant figure from his past.
4. Countertransference of the therapist towards the transference of the client. That is, the therapist is entangled by the client's transference and responds according to that interactive model.

5. Information coming from the Knowing Field, communicating to the therapist the existence of unconscious, removed contents belonging to the client or excluded members of her family system.

These five different activations can happen, to a greater or lesser degree, simultaneously. For the therapist at the beginning of his professional career, it is very hard to discern between them. Numbers 2, 3 and 4 are more marked in therapists who do not have an adequate professional training or have not undertaken in depth work on themselves. Only through adequate training and ongoing supervision is it possible to have the facility in recognizing what kind of resonances are being activated in the encounter with a client. In any case the therapist can always ask the client, through hypothetical and circular questions, if a specific sensation, emotions, state of mind or image has meaning for her. And he may discover that, at times, a cold shiver is just a cold shiver... and all you must do is turn of the air conditioner.

This kind of systemic-relational approach within the individual session is taken whether you use active techniques like the Individual Family Constellations, or whether you decide to work exclusively with words. The strength of such an approach consists in the ability to encourage new connections, internal and external, to favor a restructuring of reality.

THEORY

Very often I (Daniela) receive this kind of reflection from my clients: "You know, my life is exactly as it was before, nothing has changed in my daily life, and yet – I don't know why – I feel better!".

Germana (client of Daniela) is a 43-year-old woman who has suffered for years from serious depression, from which she healed some time ago after a period of therapy. Because she is now feeling some of those symptoms, she is very frightened.

"I need to feel that I have the strength to go on. I would like to separate from my husband, but the objective conditions are lacking and I'm scared that once again he will dominate me and gamble all our money. I can't see any solutions. My son (who is already 28) is a good son, understands everything, and now he can protect me from my husband's violent moments, but my mother is also with us: we are in her house. My dream is to have my own apartment."

During our sessions Germana came to understand better the relational entanglements that caused her to slip into a way of reacting that was apathetic, and like that of a victim. She slowly regained strength and confidence in her capacities, but most of all she started to smile again among her girlfriends, to go out occasionally with her mother, like two good friends, she took legal action to protect herself from her husband's gambling debts, and... "my life is like it was before, but I feel better, strong, and now my husband, or rather, the father of my son, sticks to the conditions I dictate... and the dream is simply postponed, but very present in me."

Individual Systemic Interview

All that we know of ourselves and of those around us constitutes "our reality" and this means it is not possible to refer to an absolute truth to choose one description rather than another. When an "external point of reference" for establishing of truth is missing, you can do no other than base yourself on the dialogue between multiple realities, which emerge in communication, in the search for a consensus.

If used at the right moment and in the right way, a technique of the Family Constellations becomes a concrete experience that allows you to go more deeply than in verbal narration, and it becomes that "external point of reference" that permits you to change the usual way of seeing and experiencing things. These techniques, therefore, are an effective means for removing the client from her usual descriptions and letting her see things differently.

This is the reason we (Marco and Daniela), besides using verbal and nonverbal communication for helping clients to "restructure" their representation of reality, have integrated these techniques into the methodology of our work.

The Individual Constellations can be considered a "representative presentification" in which the members of the family enter the therapeutic setting, taking form through one of the techniques.

When we deem it useful and constructive, we suggest that the client creates her own staging to represent some

THEORY

significant relationships (with dolls, sheets of paper, etc.). With our help she can deepen her understanding of other points of view through a concrete experience in which she can see, feel, experience and reflect in a new way on her interpersonal relations, thus forming new meanings, finding the solution to her own problems, and initiating a process of change.

Wisdom

by Bert Hellinger

The sage agrees to the world as it is,
without fear and without aims.

He is reconciled with transience
and does not aim at what passes.

He keeps an overview, because he is in harmony,
and wades in the flow of life in a simple way.

He can discern: get it or don't get it,
because he does not need to do it.

Wisdom is the fruit of discipline and practice,
but he who has it, uses it effortlessly.

He is always on the way and reaches the aim,
not because he is seeking.
He is growing.

(Hellinger, 2006; transl. by M. Moretti)

PART TWO
Practice

Individual Family Constellations

by Marco Moretti and Daniela Poggioli

Family therapy, unlike psychoanalysis, arises as a movement with various centers, many points of origin, many developments, at times interconnected but often independent. It has always been essentially plural, due to therapists having disparate theoretical bases: there are the restless, heterodox psychoanalysts, experimental family theorists, educators, social workers, anthropologists, communication theorists, and later, the behavior therapists, cognitive psychologists, and so on.

In each of these pioneers the intention was, and still is, to identify cognitive structures, techniques and therapeutic methods that are more effective than the intra-psychic approach, above all in cases of grave emotional, mental and behavioral disturbances that directly involve both the individual and her family context.

Family Therapy is the set of all intervention models that aim (albeit following diverse theories, practices and techniques) at treating (in the sense of both "healing" and "caring for") families rather than individuals, by working on their emotional and cognitive interactions (Bertrando and Toffanetti, 2000).

PRACTICE

For many years Bert Hellinger's Family Constellations have been represented in group workshops lasting one or more days, just as Hellinger himself has always done. In his original approach, the Family Constellation is in fact a psychological technique of group work.

Unlike Family Therapy, the presence of the whole family – or of all those involved in the interpersonal problem presented by client – is not necessary. It is sufficient that the client be present and ready to represent the situation she wishes to understand and resolve. Nevertheless, in time situations have arisen and have inspired a diversification of this technique, working with just the individual. The reasons are twofold:

- Many clients are not disposed to participate in a group workshop, but prefer to work one to one with the therapist.
- Many therapists prefer to work individually rather than lead groups.

These circumstances have led some therapists to use the Family Constellations in the individual setting: The Individual Family Constellations.

A technique like the Individual Family Constellations already existed from 1978. It is called *Familienbrett*, was inspired by Thea Schönfelder and developed by Kurt

Ludewig, a German psychotherapist (Ludewig *et al.*, 1983; Ludewig *et al.*, 2000). It arose from the idea of transferring Virginia Satir's technique of Family Sculptures to a usable technique in individual therapy. In the *Familienbrett* the client represents her family, or her interpersonal or work relationships, according to what she wishes to understand and resolve, arranging, as "representatives", on a 50 x 50 cm. wooden table, several wooden figures 7cm and 10cm high.

At the start of the 80's, however, the first to use the Individual Family Constellations in working with clients, according to Bert Hellinger's principles and laws, were Jakob Robert Schneider and Sieglinde Schneider (2006), two of Hellinger's collaborating counselors.

This early form of Individual Constellations was not done with wooden material as in the *Familienbrett*, but rather with Playmobil, available in Germany from 1974 (see figure 3).

> *The first time we used the Playmobil figurines to do a constellation was without even thinking about it. While at home discussing a case, we spontaneously took the figurines [no longer being used by our son], which were spread out on the floor, to represent the people we were talking about and to get some idea of this family. Thus we could look together at the family instead of just talking about it. Our perception of the problem suddenly changed. This experience sparked the question: "Why not let the clients themselves stage their*

families using the figurines?" (Schneider and Schneider, 2006).

Figure 3 – www.aufstellungsfiguren.de

The choice to use Playmobil, besides the "casual" element just described, came about because the figurines are very fetching and diverse, and clients can choose them based on shape, color and size, thus giving substance to the images most suited to the people and relationships they want to represent. Furthermore, unlike the *Familienbrett*, the figurines are identifiable as male or female, child or adult, and in the representation it is clear whom they are facing and to whom they are turning their backs.

As early as 1951 the psychoanalyst Gerhild von Staabs (1964) had created the *Scenotest*, a projective test for the study of personality, conflicts, interpersonal dynamics, and behavioral disturbances. It consisted of: flexible dolls – 8 adults and 8 children – animal figurines, cubes and other shiny materials, all of which the subject could use freely to represent scenes from her family life.

The use of dolls encourages a return to the dimension of play, and as Donald Winnicott would say, to the creation of a transitional space.

> *Psychotherapy takes place in the overlap of two areas of playing, that of the patient and that of the therapist. Psychotherapy has to do with two people playing together. The corollary of this is that where playing is not possible then the work done by the therapist is directed towards bringing the patient from a state of not being able to play into a state of being able to play (Winnicott, 1971).*

Nowadays various techniques are available for representing family members or other interpersonal relationships in individual sessions: besides dolls you can use sheets of paper or other objects, such as cushions, or free space, in which the client may move about and imagine taking different roles here and there; or you can create staging and movement in a mental space using visualization.

When, which, how and why to use one of these techniques

It is well to point out the difference existing between [psychological] techniques and exercises and between both of them and methods.
A technique can be regarded as a specific psychological procedure used in order to produce a definite effect on some aspect or function of the psyche.
An exercise consists in the combination or association of various techniques in order to produce a more general effect. [...] A method is a combination of techniques and exercises used in a specific succession or alternation according to a definite program in order to achieve the therapeutic or educational aim [...] (Assagioli, 1965).

For the therapist, psychological techniques are like the tools in a gardener's tool box. One is not a good therapist because he has a lot of "tools", but because he knows how to use them with sensibility, competence and wisdom within a therapeutic plan: he acts to increase the client's chances of choosing for herself, keeping in mind that every client is a unique being, and that the various phases of therapy or counseling are different, indeed sometimes at odds with one another.

> *Therefore, the use of a specific technique or exercise which may prove useful in one case or in one phase may be unsuitable or even harmful for other individuals, or in different conditions. [...] As therapists, then, we should, while utilizing to the full all existing techniques, constantly bear in mind that they, per se, are not enough [...]. [And above all because of the] central, decisive importance of the existential situation and problems, of the human factor and the living inter-personal relation between the therapist and the patient (Assagioli, 1965).*

When do we (Marco and Daniela) use the Individual Family Constellations? We try to understand the need, the tolerance capacity, and the right timing for the client within her specific journey. Furthermore, we try to understand which technique to use and to what end. Sometimes we may use one of these techniques in the first session, perhaps merely mentioning it, and sometimes we never use it. With some clients it may happen that one of the techniques of Individual Constellations is repeated at various moments in the therapeutic process, or it may be that once is enough. As we shall see in the next chapters, the Individual Constellations are very diverse, and what may be easy for some clients may be unworkable for others.

In all cases what must count are the principles of usefulness and harmlessness, in other words, when we suggest a certain technique to a client at a moment in her journey, it must be useful to her, must not hinder or harm her in any way, and must foster her growth.

Before using any psychological technique, moreover, we try to build what is called a "therapeutic alliance" with clients: a relationship of trust that makes for a fruitful collaboration. The premature use of any active technique can in fact compromise the therapeutic alliance, as it can bring to light intolerable aspects that may make the client feel overwhelmed. And if the client does not have enough trust in the therapist, she may decide, and often does, to break off the therapeutic relationship.

> When I (Marco) was still a novice one of my clients wanted to resolve a question to do with the inheritance left her by her parents: the family home. The property, now belonging to the two daughters, was the object of discord between the sisters. My client accused her sister of not wanting to reach a compromise that might resolve the situation. Thus, in the first session, we represented her, the sister, and the family home. From the Constellation it emerged that the family home expressed itself in the words of the mother (in fact the house had previously belonged to the mother's family) and it related to the sisters as if it were the mother. So when the mother was placed on the scene too, she said that she had deliberately left to the daughters the burden of deciding what to do with the house, because she wanted them to learn to approach each other in a mature way and to grow. From the Constellation it

also emerged that both daughters were jealous of each other and each wanted to take possession of the house, just as they used to rival each other for their mother when they were little.

My client kept blaming her sister, categorically refused to consider the possibility that she may have been jealous of her, and got angry with me for not helping her resolve the situation. It was the first and last time I ever saw her.

These days, for various reasons, many clients want fast solutions. Sometimes this is possible, but very often you need to prepare the ground and change happens step by step.

Luisella (client of Marco) is in love with a boy, but cannot decide to enter a relationship with him, even though he has been courting her for some time. At the third session I consider she is ready to explore the problem more deeply. So we represent her and the other. He shows a lot of love and eagerness towards her. She is blocked: if she approaches him, she feels growing anxiety, if she moves away, she feels pain and cries. In this stalemate appears the image of her father, whom she deeply loved when she was little, but by whom she felt betrayed and abandoned after his separation from her mother. Luisella cannot handle the intensity of these emotions, so we stop. We talk about what happened, I help her to reflect and understand. At the next session she says she does not wish to do this kind of representation anymore, because it makes her feel unhappy, but says it is fine to continue talking. At the end of the session she tells me she would like to resolve the situation in a hurry because all her girlfriends have boyfriends and she does not...

The work with Family Constellations can bring out a great deal of material for elaboration, and despite the client's being eager to resolve her problems, it is still necessary to create a basis of awareness and containment so that what emerges may be tolerable, comprehensible, acceptable, and worked through, in other words, the emerging material must help her to know, possess and transform the situation.

In Luisella's case, I (Marco) would have been able to end the Constellation with some ritual sentence, as you often make people say in group Constellations, for example: "You show me my destiny", or "This is still my place", or "Not for you, but for him", and so on. But I (Marco) believe that a phrase that's too distant from what the client feels or thinks in a given moment may be useless or even harmful. A ritual sentence must in some way rouse the client, but at the same time it must have meaning, must be comprehensible and restructuring, that is, it must be felt, and must help the client become aware of her situation and contribute to its restructuring. In Luisella's case I felt it opportune to end the representation and discuss with her what had emerged; I did not want to overburden her, and wanted to safeguard the therapeutic alliance, which, in later sessions, allowed us to go on with the work and resolve the problem.

Individual Family Constellations

Another aspect to consider is the fact that the use of techniques tends to make the client passive. Often the client comes to a session with the expectation that the therapist will resolve the situation. Much more in Family Constellations, known for their efficacy, clients expect to resolve quickly the problem they are presenting. Nevertheless, experience shows that wanting change is not enough for it to happen: one must also be willing to assume responsibility for it. A technique is therefore useful when the client can assume responsibility and the "cost" of change, to become an active part of this process. What are the signs that the therapist may pick up? There are at least three: the capacity to reflect and gain greater awareness of the problem, and of what a change implies, and the capacity to make decisions about this. Otherwise the Family Constellations becomes a kind of little drama that does not open new possibilities of understanding and choice.

To summarize, before using a technique of the Individual Constellations we establish with the client a relationship of trust, understanding and collaboration. From the start we try to follow her vital interest, what she feels and what is most important to her. In the way the client tells us about herself and her relationships, we try to gather and reflect the phrases and gestures that have the greatest emotional charge. When the client expounds a problem or distress she is experiencing, through bodily empathy, mirroring and reformulation of her communications, we help her to focus and express clearly her deep wish, and to connect her body, vital energy, emotions, mind and soul. Thus the client and her Constellation gain strength and vitality. If instead the client is left to herself, she will tend to become inhibited and sink into the vicious circle of her habitual stories. In that way she and her Constellation will lose strength and vitality.

Which technique of the Individual Constellations should we use? Each therapist, based on his professional approach and methodologies, has his preferred techniques. A good therapist ought to have thoroughly experienced on himself all the techniques he uses and thus acquired competence and expertise. In the Family Constellations, a therapist who uses the individual techniques should at any rate have participated in many workshops of group Family Constellations and have worked in depth on himself, both in group and individually, with various Constellation techniques and therapies. And all this requires humility, patience, experimentation, continual training, and supervision.

Daniela, for instance, uses the Systemic-Relational methodology, Gestalt and Individual Constellation techniques using dolls. Marco on the other hand uses Biosystemic psycho-bodily techniques, the methodology and techniques of Psychosynthesis, group and individual Family Constellations with sheets of paper, space and visualizations.

Individual Family Constellations

From our experience we have noticed that the clients who have participated in a lot of group Family Constellations workshops, are much more receptive, open and able to use many techniques of the Individual Constellations. In our opinion this is because the group Family Constellations enhance flexibility and expansion of consciousness, thus helping people to develop greater psychological and interpersonal functional plasticity. In any case we have the possibility of using various techniques just for meeting the needs and capacities of clients: the use of dolls, sheets of paper, free space, and visualization.

In the following sections we have arranged these different techniques of Individual Constellations in order of difficulty, from greater concreteness to greater abstractness.

The technique of the dolls is the most usable because the most concrete. The client simply chooses and arranges the dolls on the table and, with the therapist's help, reflects on the representation as on a question that involves her but that she can observe from outside. The representation with dolls does not involve the bodily plane, and allows the client to stay on the plane of reflection when the therapist sees that it is better not to go too deeply into the emotions. If, on the other hand, the client is ready to go more into the work, the therapist can ask her to imagine the sensations, emotions and states of mind of the various figures represented, and what happens when she places the dolls in one way or another. With this technique the Knowing Field expresses itself above all through the therapist's receptivity, and can touch the client with his words and with his sensibility in changing the dolls' positions; however it can manifest also through the client, to the extent that she is able to identify with the various figures represented.

The technique that uses the sheets of paper, on which is written the name and role of the figure represented, is more experiential than that of the dolls because it allows the client to move to each one of these in turn, and to explore what the various members of the system feel. Compared to the former technique, this one permits the client to be more fully immersed in the Knowing Field. However, it does not produce good results if the client is too bent on thought at the expense of sensations and emotions, or if she is "self-referential", that is, too rigid and subjective in her thinking and tending to refer everything to herself and neglect the other points of view.

These first two techniques permit you easily to enter and leave the experience of the representation, so it is possible to proceed to the end of the representation as well as to temporarily interrupt it for the sake of discussion and to return and immerse yourself in it again. With the next two techniques, however, it is unadvisable to interrupt and resume them in the same session because they presuppose greater contemplation and involvement, which is better maintained from start to finish.

The technique of free space – where the representation is constructed slowly in space, the client imagining the presence of other figures – is more dynamic than the previous one because the represented figures can be pictured in interactive movement, and therefore, as an experience it resembles more what happens in group Constellations. This technique allows you to enter deeply into the Knowing Field, but demands of the client great receptivity, and plenty of openness to sensations, emotions, and the imaginative function. In fact, with this technique you can have access to images that come directly from the Knowing Field, and literally to see scenes from the past being represented before the client's, and at times also the therapist's, eyes.

The technique of visualization works like that of free space, but all is represented mentally through the imagination. The client is seated with eyes closed, visualizes a scene in which are present the figures of the represented system, and during the work, she can enter and leave the various images of the characters, with the aim of feeling and experiencing the different sensations and emotions, dialoguing with the other figures, and so forth. This technique acts so in depth that the client may go into states of trance. But it is also the hardest to practice, as few clients can visualize vividly and at length.

PRACTICE

The hardest part of the work with the [Individual] Constellations lies in the therapist's or counselor's capacity to perceive the deepest processes of the soul in a system of relationships (Schneider and Schneider, 2006).

This skill can be honed thanks to the experience as representative in the group Family Constellations. Therapists who have participated in many group Constellations are in fact better able to "see" and perceive what manifests in the Knowing Field. This aspect is very important because in individual work the therapist must already have learned to "see" and "feel" the different and complex interpersonal dynamics.

In the individual setting the therapist or counselor obtains much of this information through observing the client. For this reason it is crucial, during the whole session and even more during the Individual Constellation, to pay attention to the client's bodily movements, gestures, facial expressions, tone of voice, breathing, and further, to the direction of her movements, gestures and glances, and to the form, rhythm and intensity of all these manifestations in the relationship between her and us, and between her and the other figures in her family system.

What are the mistakes a therapist may commit in conducting an Individual Constellation? Let us look at some of them:

Individual Family Constellations

1. Concentrating too much on what to do, on the technical aspects or the representation, thus losing sight of the client and not tuning into her and to the Knowing Field.
2. Following his own idea or "what would be the right thing to do", without keeping in mind the client's real needs and degree of awareness.
3. Not gleaning the client's vital interest and heart's desire, and thus undertaking the work of Constellation without vital energy.
4. Suggesting a technique that's unsuitable for the client or badly timed.
5. Giving excessive importance to a piece of information while neglecting another, or becoming confused by much information.

At the end of a session, how can we tell if an Individual Constellation has had a good result?

Even if at the end of the individual session the client does not yet know what effect the experience will have, she should still feel in herself an increase of strength and a certain confidence (Schneider and Schneider, 2006).

Besides this, at best, she may feel a sense of relief, openness of heart, serenity, joy, a sense of perspective and freedom. We can notice all that from the relaxation in the face, brightness in the eyes, better breathing, and a change in posture. At worst, she should at least have greater clarity, motivation and sense of responsibility.

At the end of the session, it is useful to consolidate these positive states of mind and help the client be aware of them: summarizing the themes treated, asking her how she feels, and "what she is taking home" in the way of new hypotheses on which to work.

Limitations and advantages of the Individual Family Constellations

Like all psychological techniques, the Individual Constellations have their limits. Let's examine them, compared to the group Constellations:

1. The limited scope of the Knowing Field.
2. The lack of energy, dynamism and Gestalt typical of the group. In fact the group has the power to manifest overall the form and dynamism of the whole represented system, bringing out more easily the implicit dynamics of the system.
3. The group Constellation is more "convincing" and immediate for the client because it is the representatives themselves who show the different behaviors of each member.

Individual Family Constellations

4. Less depth and emotional participation than that experienced in group.
5. A necessary simplification of the representation means that the Individual Constellations are, for one reason or another, less "unsettling" than the group ones.

The Family Constellations are generally not advisable for those who:

- Do not want to treat family or interpersonal themes.
- Cannot consider themselves, what they feel, and their experience, in a relation of interdependence with the family system.
- Are not interested in, or ready to perceive within themselves, their emotional ties.
- Do not trust a phenomenological and systemic approach.

The Individual Constellations also have some advantages. For the therapist they are:

1. The possibility of knowing the client in depth, thus undertaking more targeted work.
2. The ease of conducting the Individual Constellation, because fewer variables are at play than in the group situation.

PRACTICE

3. Greater tolerability of the therapeutic work, because you can treat one theme at a time. There is also the possibility of exploring in a few sessions the various dynamics of the system, the ties and alliances between members of the family, and all that binds and connects them in destiny's story.
4. Less fatigue because it is easier to lead an Individual Constellation than a group one.

The advantages for the client are:

1. The chance for an individual exchange with the therapist, therefore more available attention and time.
2. Greater freedom in sharing because it is easier to trust one therapist than a group of people.
3. Greater possibility for tolerating emotionally the therapeutic work, both because the individual representation is simplified with respect to that of the group, and because the work can be diluted through several sessions and by going into one theme at a time.
4. Economic saving, since an Individual Constellation costs less than a group workshop.

The Silent Helpers: Use of the Dolls
By Daniela Poggioli

I first saw the Playmobil figurines used by Sieglinde Schneider in September 2002 in Trieste. In a 3-day workshop Sieglinde gave us a demonstration of Individual Constellations using the colored Playmobils, presenting a simple and direct way of transferring the group Constellations work to the individual setting. Still dazed by my first experience of group Constellations, I could not imagine how the Playmobils could be used in individual consultation. I approached the table where Sieglinde was. She asked who among the participants wanted to do an individual work. A woman offered to do it: she wished to know why the relationship with her husband was not satisfying and why she often felt almost a stranger with him.

Sieglinde spread the Playmobils on the table and suggested the client create a scene, taking one figurine for representing her husband, one for herself, and two for her parents, according to the perception she had of her relations with these family members.

The Playmobils, immobile and silent, staged in a scene, began to evoke slightly confused and disorganized family scenes, and slowly and delicately, the leader accompanied the woman in her observation of the representation, suggesting other possible positions of the characters, putting each representative in his or her appropriate place, thus transforming the initial scene.

The work lasted little more than twenty minutes and was of surprising efficacy – moving and enlightening – compared to the inner perception the woman had of her parents: she had placed herself near her mother and father, looking at her husband but not with her husband. From this first scene, Sieglinde helped the woman find her place in the hierarchical order and her role as wife, defining each step with ritual sentences.

The Playmobil that represented the client was placed in front of the parent Playmobils and Sieglinde made the woman say: "Dear parents, thank you for the life you have given me, I honor you! I will make something good of my life! This is my husband".

In the new configuration, husband and wife were facing each other and the phrase Sieglinde made the woman say was: "My dear husband, I have not been very present for you, but now I see you and I am here as a wife to you!". She made the husband say: "Dear wife, I have been waiting for you a long time and now I welcome you with love".

The final or decisive scene had the same four colored Playmobils, but all who observed the different steps along with the client were aware of having witnessed a story without words and at the same time a story known and "experienced".

The Silent Helpers: Use of the Dolls

Through the years and in many workshops, I have witnessed other experiences of individual sessions with the figurines, sheets of paper on the floor, colored clothing arranged on the floor, use of objects for representing the family members, and I have been able to learn and gain much information and appreciate its efficacy and validity for doing good work in individual sessions.

Even if I have seen that it's irrelevant which dolls are chosen, I shall nevertheless give a few useful criteria:

1. The size of the figurines have to be such that you can carry them with you anywhere and move them easily on a table.
2. The work will be easier if the figurines are distinctly male and female and show the direction of their gaze, or at least whom they are facing and to whom they have their back turned.
3. The fewer their features and the less they attract attention, the better. Some therapists love dolls that make certain associations and therefore interpretations possible: figurines of animals or characteristic dolls. But the work with the group constellations shows how important in phenomenological work it is that the facilitator does not let himself be guided by associations and peculiar characteristics, except in a limited way, and that she avoids everything which takes her attention away from the essential events, destinies and relational dynamics. The figurines, like the representatives in a group, don't represent single characters in themselves, but rather the plane on which are projected members of the client's family or her other relational systems, of which she has or has not had

PRACTICE

experience. They reflect also a field of relation in space, which usually does not depend on the people's outer appearance.
4. *It has been shown to be useful that the dolls distinguish children from adults when children who either died young or were lost through miscarriage or abortion are represented.*
5. *It is also most useful to be able to distinguish the dolls by their colors when placing large systems in a scene. Whereas the group constellations draw much energy from the strength and concentrated attention of the group – which sometimes indicates when attention is deviating from the essential – the constellation with the dolls lacks this support. It allows you to place on the scene many family members. For example, in couples counseling, you can put both the wife's and the husband's families. Or, depending on how things are going in the consultation, you can consider the essential destinies in the families of both parents. So our Playmobil figurines allow us to distinguish, through color, the mother's and the father's families. This facilitates the orientation (Schneider and Schneider, 2006).*

Considering the above criteria, I went to a learning center and found wooden dolls (not Playmobil), divided into families with the suggested physical features of grandparents, children and grandchildren (see figure 4). I bought four families, which have been with me in a lovely, colored box in my studio for many years.

The Silent Helpers: Use of the Dolls

Figure 4

The introduction of the dolls in the session, individual or couple, almost never happens in the first encounters, except when a specific consultation in Individual Family Constellations is requested because the person does not want to talk about her problems in front of a group; in such cases I use the dolls, but make sure I point out that the limitation of this technique is that it doesn't show the strength of the "Knowing Field", which is activated especially with the representatives in flesh and bone.

The technique of the dolls is practiced by many counselors and therapists. I have developed it in a gradual process, combining it with my systemic-relational training. I have attended hundreds of Constellations workshops with different leaders, while carrying on my clinical work, begun in the 90's. I have gained much experience through family therapy training, and later through being a representative in Constellations workshops.

Being a representative is like experiencing a kind of waking trance, where your senses are active and deeply concentrated on perceiving something different to what you can understand: there exist experiences and relationships with unconscious dynamics that are hard to see. To put yourself in another's shoes, just for the time of a representation, is a way of understanding experiences that are often unknown to us. For someone like me, whose job is the healing of relationships, this is essential.

In individual sessions with the dolls, I can draw from all that and lead the client into a concentration that avoids the tendency to "skirt around the problem", and that

> *[...] shows her in an often direct and enlightening way that the context of the problem, as too the desired solution, must be contemplated differently to how it was before (Schneider and Schneider, 2006).*

Thus, when I observe the scene with the dolls, the Knowing Field enters play through me, and so I can ask for more specific information on the various family relationships: what alliances have been formed, what exclusions or injustices have occurred through the generations, which events have most marked the families, and so on. In this way the story expands and doors are opened to new hypotheses that stimulate progressive dynamics and processes. The satisfaction in seeing a new configuration of the reality is revealed in the breathing, mine and the client's, and in her serene and often smiling expression.

Placing these dolls before a person, creating scenes and observing them together, offers an image that is often unpredictable but easily accessible and shared. Furthermore, the acted out, rather than the spoken, is more effective in expressing something inside us, without too much mental interference.

I wish to point out that in the individual Constellations sessions with the dolls, it is the therapist or counselor who "animates" the representations, who becomes representative for each subject and who tells his or her story and the relational plots, thanks to the phenomenological knowledge acquired in the groups.

The "silent helpers" have never disappointed me.

How I proceed

I use the dolls both with single clients and with couples. With the individual client I use them after having established a relationship of trust and an atmosphere of empathy. I take the box and open it in front of the person, and I present my

PRACTICE

"silent helpers", who are often received with surprise and a sincere smile.

I take the dolls and give them to the client, and ask her to create a scene on the table by placing them in relation to one another according to her inner perception of the significant relationships.

We both look at the scene, and I always ask: "What do you see?", "How does this arrangement look to you?" and from that moment the dolls command our attention: they are observed, touched, moved in space, or moved from the relationship and observed again. Thus a seemingly simple but extremely delicate, calibrated and efficacious work takes place. Seeing and looking at the relationships stimulates much reflection by the client, and stimulates in me circular questions that bring into play new relational possibilities.

Often people come to therapy or counseling loaded with blame or guilt, reproach and anger for what could have been avoided. Systemic and Constellations work removes them from blaming because the question is not: whose fault is it? But: what can have occurred in that relationship, what kind of tie has been created through time, and what intentions have been misunderstood.

The benevolent effect of this method becomes more evident in couples sessions, where the partners come already full of resentment, mutual reproach, anger and irreversible disappointments.

The Silent Helpers: Use of the Dolls

Through the methods of the Constellations, the situation soon relaxes, as the couple can see how both, in their behavior, are tied to the destinies of their own family, and can see which old patterns each is repeating in the reciprocal relationship, what each is contributing to the conflict, how little the other is seen in the conflict, what the other is really like, and how much, despite these disturbed behaviors, they are made for each other (Schneider and Schneider, 2006).

Many times in therapy clients and couples have given positive feedback on this way of working with the dolls and how they have internalized and re-elaborated the represented scenes according to the concept of "relational circularity", and how they have reconsidered their own responsibilities in the conflicts and transference projections.

For many people the visual aspect is more efficacious than the verbal, and this provides a set of information that enhances the process of change.

In general the technique of the dolls may be used with anyone, but the effectiveness is better with an educational and therapeutic basis of trust and sensibility.

For years I have noticed that the kind of client who comes to me, as to many of my colleagues, is informed, aware, and has often had experience with other therapies, which means the request is more demanding and more focused on specific subjects.

PRACTICE

By including the Systemic Constellations in therapeutic journeys of different approaches, we can respond with considerable success to this kind of request, and help the client move on.

In couples sessions I use the dolls in a double stage set-up, where I observe and check particularly important points:

- Who shows greater authority and dominance and speaks for both?
- Is there blame or contempt between the partners?
- Is there balance of give and take in the relationship?
- The quality of attachment of each to his or her parent of the same sex.
- Which of the two original families exerts more control or pressure?
- In which original system have there been dramatic events?
- Is there respect for the partner's family of origin?

The silent helpers are very useful right from the first sessions, as they show me straightaway which family of origin has more suffering, and what kind of relationship the couple has built: symmetric, complementary, conflicting, punishing, and so on.

I place in both members' hands the dolls that represent each, and ask: "Both of you create a scene that represents your inner perception of the couple, not the ideal couple you would like".

Often the two scenes are very different: this for a start is interesting information that surprises the couple (not me), and despite their suffering and frustration also makes them smile.

In the scenes with the dolls you often see the difference in the partners' two systems of origin, above all you see if one system is more disorganized than the other. For example, if one of the two constructs a scene in which the parents are far from each other or facing opposite directions, or the grandparents are placed in the foreground with respect to the parents, or there are many dead among the extended family, then I have direct information to take as a starting point for an in-depth investigation.

The connections between the two systems of origin help to clarify which familial patterns are repeated, which redundancies recur, which original ties are reflected in the couple, and what expectations exist.

In couples therapy I follow the systemic approach that offers therapies – brief in number, but spread over time, that is, monthly or bimonthly at the beginning – and the method of the dolls is an extra resource for identifying, in a short time, the systemic disorders that have contributed to the failure of the relationship.

PRACTICE

Marco and Alice

One day I receive a phone call from Alice, who confusedly requests an appointment for her and her husband "because something is amiss... But then again, something has always been amiss, so there's no hurry!".

Alice and Marco have been married for 13 years and have an 11-year-old boy. They are both about 40, she works in a small firm, while he, after several jobs, has had growing success and manages an electronic equipment company.

When I first meet them we introduce ourselves, and as I always do with couples, I ask each to tell me the problem from his or her point of view.

After a brief introduction of the problems I suggest working with my "silent helpers" to identify the interlocking relational configuration that have developed, or the way in which the two parties either sustain the couple or conflict with each other.

Marco and Alice create two completely different scenes: he places the two dolls side by side, whereas Alice places them far apart.

In such cases it is obvious that the woman carries the emotional burden of the suffering, and after a short observation, I ask Alice: "How long have you felt this distance between you?" the woman starts to cry and the husband, confused and embarrassed, looks at her.

The Silent Helpers: Use of the Dolls

Alice relates a few dramas that involved her family. She felt a moral duty to take care of her mother, distancing herself more and more from her husband, who in turn did not understand how much his wife was suffering and felt abandoned.

I shan't expound the various steps of the process, because it would require a whole chapter, but it is interesting to see how the use of the dolls, within the Constellations perspective, allows us straightaway to zero in on the problem.

By what criteria can I define one scene more problematic than another?

I refer to the Orders of Love, which are Hellinger's empirical deductions from years of observing the practice of Family Constellations groups. They describe:

- The power of time and of space: the generational hierarchy has an influence on the whole system and on those who come afterwards.
- The "debts" of one generation fall on the next one if they are not closed and resolved.
- The Orders make no provision for morals, but are at the service of the system: they give priority to the group over the individual, to biology over mind, and include profound differences between the genders.

PRACTICE

For example, in the above case with the leader Sieglinde, the client places in the scene herself, her parents and her husband without respecting a certain order: her position as an adult and wife cannot be near her parents, as this implies staying in her family of origin and not respecting the new nucleus formed when a woman chooses to marry her partner.

Another example: if a 19-year-old son puts himself in between his parents, you have a scene unsuited to the boy's age. From such a placement it seems the boy is not developing his independence and we would need to explore with him whether the position is for protecting the parents, himself, or whether he has remained interlock in a "triangulation", that is, whether he is standing in for one of his parents.

Yet another example: A woman is the fourth of six children, and in the scene she creates she places herself far from everyone with her back to the family, the siblings all aligned with the parents. What is happening? This kind of scene is problematic, and the first step is to ask the woman: "What grave event happened in the family, including the other generations?". We should recognize with which member of the family she is allied, or from whom she is running away, or whether she has become entangled with someone who has been excluded.

The Silent Helpers: Use of the Dolls

Gianni: son or husband?

Gianni is a 43-year-old man, good looking though somewhat subdued and slightly overweight. He lives in Bologna with his wife and a 5-year-old child. He has been sent to me by his wife, whose friend, an ex-client of mine, gave her my name.

His request is to help him improve the relationship with his wife because since the birth of their baby, whom he perhaps wanted more than she did, he and his wife have not been getting along.

I ask Gianni: "But if it is a problem of the couple, why don't you come together?". He answers that his wife can't stand his laziness anymore, that she has done her bit, now it's his turn.

During the session Gianni clearly shows physical embarrassment: he touches his arms, scratches his head and nose, often looks down, and continuously shifts about in his chair.

He answers questions with caution and effort, and gradually I realize that his embarrassment in facing me comes from being unaware of his own emotions and unaccustomed to introspection.

His original family's story shows a crucial drama: his father died in an accident at work at the age of 25 when Gianni's mother was pregnant with him. Gianni never knew his father and was raised by his mother and maternal grandparents, and later by his mother's new partner, whom he calls Dad.

His wife Carla complains that he is unavailable to her and their only child, and criticizes Gianni especially for his laziness, low self-esteem, and his mother's interference in their relationship, even after her death. The sessions with Gianni proceed regularly but with few results; nevertheless, he proves to be confident in therapy, despite serious regressions that throw him and the relationship with his wife into crisis.

The therapeutic turning point happens during a session with my "silent helpers". I ask Gianni to place in a scene himself and his mother. The scene is Gianni with his mother facing him. We observe the scene and both of us know someone is missing. I take a doll that represents his biological father, and see that Gianni's eyes are teary. He is hesitant in picking up the father's representative, and when he does, he holds his breath and quickly places it next to his Mum.

We look at the scene again and I have a clear intuition: Gianni has been not only his mother's son but also her "husband".

The ethical question for me is how to translate this intuition so that he can use it.

I wait a bit, allow the scene to develop its "field", and slowly suggest a small shift, saying: "How do you see the scene if your father and mother face and look at each other while you observe them?". I make the small change... and see Gianni lean against the back of the chair and breathe a sigh of relief. The scene is quite clear, shows order in the relations, and above all, releases Gianni from his mother's "spell".

The Knowing Field's function acts through the dolls too, and is highlighted in nonverbal signs, like a change in breathing, posture, and flow of the emotions.

In subsequent sessions, Gianni has continued to work on this scene: he is more present for his wife Carla and has arranged to go on an outing alone with his son.

The therapy is still in progress.

Sara: I want my consistency

Sara is 40-years-old woman and has a serious, urgent problem: she wants to separate from her husband even though she has two small children, one two years, the other 8 months.

No one knows she wants to separate. She is sure, but doesn't know how to make her husband understand, nor her parents, whom she has never disobeyed.

PRACTICE

She has been living for some time in a state of anguish that is taking away her appetite and making her react to her family with angry outbursts. She often cries by herself, and sleeps little.

In the first session Sara tells the story of her marriage in 2008 to her high school boyfriend, a serious and good boy, well-mannered and reliable. The union has been well accepted by both families, and both members of the couple are adored and loved only children.

Sara, besides her loving family, has a small group of sisterly friends, in whom she trusts and confides.

But Sara is not comfortable with herself because she knows how she is inside and does not like it. She has developed the habit of lying to reassure her parents, yet she doesn't like that either.

In a session I ask her to create a scene with two identical dolls, one for Sara and one for the other Sara, and I have them carry on a dialogue.

Sara is a little surprised and reluctant, but she calmly commits herself to it, and out comes a host of mutual judgments and prejudices. After fifteen minutes of moderate conflict (moderate in tone), Sara moves the two dolls so they have their backs to each other… It seems they do not want to see each other, so I ask her: "What is happening in this last scene?". "What's happening is that they don't get along and they both stick to their guns. I turned them round so they don't have to face each other!".

We close the session and Sara leaves, visibly upset.

In our next meetings Sara wants to talk about her relationship with her father and how angry she is with him.

Many years ago, when Sara was twenty, she overheard a phone call between her father and a woman, and from the familiar, intimate tone, quickly understood that the woman was not her mother. It hurt Sara a great deal, and she did not tell anyone: thus, she was her father's accomplice. Her father saw that his daughter knew, but reassured her, saying no other woman existed besides her mother. It did not reassure Sara, who harbored much bitterness and disappointment. For the first time Sara encountered emotional ambivalence: how could her father betray his wife's trust and tell his daughter such gross lies? This wonderful and good father was cohabiting with a wicked traitor.

What is more, Sara knew, though wished she didn't, that her mother was suffering from all this: what a cage and what inconsistency.

This new awareness makes Sara a bit stronger, surer of her feelings and less afraid of her family's judgment.

In the next session I again suggest we work with the "silent helpers" and place in her hands 4 dolls that represent her own family and 2 that represent her parents, using the three-generation criterion (grandparent dolls, parent dolls, children dolls) and I ask her: "What place do you give each one of them?".

Sara concentrates a while, takes a deep breath, quickly places herself and her children in the scene, and thinks... She doesn't know where to put her husband. She tries a few positions, places him near her, near the children, then picks him up again, and finally puts him near, but not too near, the children, and looking at them. This new arrangement pleases her, she smiles and says: "Yes, this is fine because he is a good father, but not a good husband for me. But yes, he's a good father!".

Now she has the parents to place in position.

Sara decisively puts them behind her as protection for her and her children, not as close to her as she thought, but a few centimeters away.

At the end Sara relaxes, smiles and looks with satisfaction at the scene: "Yes, I like it, all have a good place. I feel at peace."

We say goodbye before the summer break and make an appointment for September.

And at the September meeting she has much news: Sara has spoken with her husband, with her mother, who had already been aware of her daughter's unhappiness, and with her father.

Her husband does not agree to separating. For him, things are fine as they are and he doesn't understand why she is discontented. Sara continues to be unhappy with him and, not wanting to battle nor to argue further, asks me if I know of a center for family counseling, where she might have some sessions with her husband.

In the next months relations remain a little tense, but they still live courteously under the same roof.

The surprise Sara has is from her father, who does not accept this separation. He becomes gloomy and tells her: "You can always take a lover if you are not happy with him. Why do you have to harm your children?". Once again her father's inconsistency emerges. She is not prepared for this reaction and gets angry. The important new factor for Sara is that she now needs to be consistent before her children. She wants to be a good mother to them, but wants a satisfying relationship with a partner.

In one of our last sessions Sara says: "You know, those dolls gave me true mental clarity. I have suffered so much because of my father's betrayal, and I think he is still having extramarital affairs, but it's their business, and I don't want to play that game. I'll take my responsibilities, but at least I feel clean and consistent in front of my children. And you know what else? I am also happier with myself!".

To sum up: in individual Constellations sessions with the dolls what is missing are the representatives, their physical sensations and sharing: the dolls are silent and stationary. It is the therapist's task to identify himself with the system of relations, to express what he "sees" represented, and describe it to the client, or identify with the scene to bring out the inner dynamics. For example: "In this scene it seems that all are on their own; how lonely they must feel!", or: "When I look at your position it seems to me as if you are living in a cage. Have you ever had this sensation?", or: "If I put your father far from everyone, somewhat on his own, who follows him and who excludes him?", and so forth.

What convinces me that this method works?

It is undoubtedly my clients' response: "How did you know my mother would have said those things?", "Yes, that's how it went!", "Now that you point it out, I understand my father's behavior better." What in systemic therapy is defined as "hypothesis", in the Family Constellations is a person's visible entanglement or identification with a preceding family member, or the closeness and loyalty she has to family members without being aware of it.

Thus a new process begins, and we therapists and counselors can enhance the steps forward, support the regressions, dry the tears when necessary, but never demand the change we would expect, because that remains the client's exclusive responsibility, with due regard for what she can or cannot change.

Use of Sheets of Paper

by Marco Moretti

I have been leading Family Constellations groups for several years, and started straight after participating in Bert Hellinger's first workshops in Italy. For a couple of years I led a fortnightly experimental group, and from 2004 I organized Family Constellations workshops for the public. As I had Psychosynthesis training, I have continued to do individual work with clients. Not all my clients participated in the group Family Constellations I led. And only with some of those who did, have I used, the techniques of Individual Constellations.

When the Family Constellations became better known, many clients started to ask if they could work individually with them. Since I was already using several similar Psychosynthesis techniques (dialogues with the subpersonalities, etc.), I decided to develop the Individual Family Constellations, using the sheets of paper, and basing the work on my previous experiences.

How I proceed

Whereas use of the dolls requires a table at least 50 x 50 cm., use of the sheets of paper requires a space of at least 3 x

PRACTICE

3 meters. As with the dolls, the client creates (though on the floor) a scene, in which the characters are represented by A4-size sheets of paper, divided in halves, with the name of the represented person written on it and an arrow drawn, showing the direction to which it is turned (see figure 5).

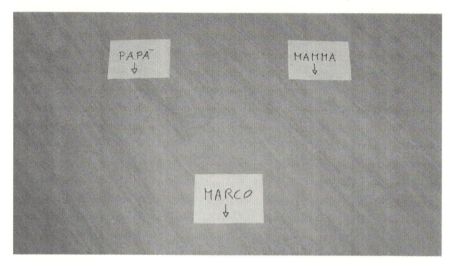

Figure 5

I prefer to use sheets of paper with names on them (rather than, for example, cushions), to identify clearly the person represented. I also find it useful to show with an arrow the direction in which the represented person is facing. This is because small movements in fact cause significant changes. The only time I don't use the arrow below a subjects' names is if they are dead, in which case I treat them as if they were supine.

Use of Sheets of Paper

Unlike the dolls, use of the sheets of paper is on the one hand more abstract, and on the other more experiential. Although in representing with sheets of paper you don't have the dynamic aspect of interactive movement, as you have in the group Constellations, nevertheless with this technique the client is more connected to the Knowing Field. This is because after creating the scene, the client may move onto each sheet of paper and "feel" what each represented figure experiences.

When do I use this technique? Rarely do I suggest it at the first session. Sometimes, though, a client will come to counseling with the intention of doing an Individual Family Constellation. In such circumstances I may use it even in the first session if the client has already worked with the Family Constellations, if a relation of trust and empathy is established between us, and if I think this technique would be useful and constructive for her. If, on the other hand, I feel the client is expecting a "miraculous" event to unblock, thanks to me or to this technique, a situation for which she cannot or will not assume responsibility, then I prefer to "disillusion" the client and work only through conversation. For the same reasons I don't apply any technique just to satisfy a client's curiosity or desire to manipulate someone. So, to avoid interference in others' lives, I do not place in the scene people with whom the client has no emotionally significant ties. However, if this is not possible – say, for example, because the client needs to do a Constellation linked to her work – I do allow representation of other figures, but avoid exploring them in depth, preferring to focus the client's attention on her established relations with the others.

I use this technique with clients who are aware, open and interested enough to explore more deeply their interpersonal relations, but most of all with those whom I deem able to tolerate and assume their part of the responsibility for what may arise. I easily use it with those who have already participated positively in group Constellations. Sometimes ex-clients return to do an Individual Constellations session, just to understanding and resolving a specific situation. In all cases I always use it in the service of goals on which the client and I have agreed together.

A Constellation with the sheets of paper is useful with clients who can listen to and recognize their own sensations and emotions and reflect on them. Otherwise it is useless and frustrating for a person who, standing on a sheet of paper that represents someone, does not feel anything or cannot give a name to what she is experiencing. This may happen to clients who are too focused on thought, or have the dysfunction called *alexithymia*, or are too centered on themselves. Clients with psychotic functioning may feel invaded by de-structuring sensations and emotions, or may distort in a delirious way what they experience in a representation.

Use of Sheets of Paper

When I feel this technique may be useful and constructive for a client, I ask her if she is interested in using it for the issue on which she wants to work. Some clients bring much material to work on: others bring less. Sometimes during the session a certain issue for exploration unfolds easily. If instead the client tends to relate contingent situations, I will, after fifteen minutes of in-depth talk (I do sessions of one hour), find it useful to ask: "What do you want to work on today?". Once I have singled out the theme that is most important to the client – the one she holds most interesting and most wishes to go into – I suggest a suitable technique for exploring it. When the issues are interpersonal, and depending on the client's typology, I propose the Individual Constellations using the sheets of paper. If the client is interested, we decide together whom to represent.

I take a few A4 sheets divided in half and write the name of the represented person or, for the parents, "Mum" or "Dad", which are the names the client uses to refer to them. I then say to the client: "Place the sheets on the floor as you perceive the relationships between you". The client thus represents a scene: she chooses an arrangement, and therefore a form, for these relations, according to the distance between the various figures and the direction in which they are facing. At this point, if it is the first time we are working together and the client has no experience of the technique, I sit next to her in front of the scene, and invite her to observe and reflect on it. It is like what happens with the dolls.

When I notice the client focused and "immersed" in the scene, I introduce her into the representation. If it is her first time with this technique, I place her in her own role on the sheet of paper with her name on it, with her legs slightly apart and the sheet between her feet. I put her in her role to avoid her becoming confused. If, on the other hand, she has already worked in this way, I may decide to put her straightaway in other roles. Then I tell her to imagine, standing here in flesh and blood, all the other represented figures. Given that the sheets of paper are placed on the floor, the client usually looks down at the ground, which is why I ask her to imagine the others standing in their positions.

The first time the client represents another figure she may have doubts about the representation, and may ask if she must pretend to relate to that character. I therefore explain from the start that it is not a role-play or psychodrama, but a representation in which she enters the bodily, emotional and mental feeling of the other – as if she were the other. Thus, when I position the client, I tell her that what she is going to feel and experience belongs to the person she is representing, and so to trust her own sensations. In this way the client makes herself receptive to the Knowing Field.

When the client is in position I take away her sheet of paper (to allow changes of position) and help her focus on the sensations and emotions. I guide her in listening to her body and to everything she feels and experiences. For a few minutes we listen to the body without speaking. I then ask what she feels in her body and what emotions she experiences. After this, I have her attend to what she experiences in relation to the other figures represented. From this moment the use of the word is subordinate to the Constellation, so if the client feels significant emotions towards a certain person, I may ask her to say – reformulating adequately what she feels – a sentence to the person concerned. For example, if the client feels pain because she is not really seen by her father, I may ask her to turn to her father and say: "When you don't see me I suffer". And I ask the client if this sentence is consonant with her experience. If it is not, we find a more suitable one together. I work in this way, exploring in depth the feeling of that represented person in relation to all the others.

In the Family Constellations, as in life, every gesture and look, every movement and all that we experience, is always in relation to someone else. Each of our expressions is by nature relational. For this reason any expressive movement that manifests in the Constellation, I always trace back to something that is happening in the represented system.

During this work the client, as representative, may feel she wants to move farther or closer to someone, or to turn around; or I will notice in her body a slight oscillation or movement of approach or distancing, so I will ask the client to follow that movement. I try to favor manifestation of the Soul's movements, and when I notice them, if the client doesn't follow them, I will invite her to do so, sometimes asking her expressly to take a step forward or backward. Straight afterwards, I will ask her if that movement feels right and if it is better for her. If the movement is authentic, it will always bring with it greater harmony. I thus help her to listen and recognize the spontaneous bodily movements activated by the Soul. I encourage these authentic movements, but not those that are in reaction or flight, which instead are connected to defensive emotions. And so gradually the scene starts to undergo a structural modification.

When the client has in this way explored a figure, I have her leave that role, I place the corresponding sheet of paper in the new position created during the work, and I put the client on another sheet of paper that represents a different person. The choice is often for the one with whom the client has greatest interpersonal difficulties. I repeat the procedure and encourage deep communication between some, if not all, of the represented figures. I continue in this way till the client has impersonated all the representatives, if it is useful, otherwise only those that have a more significant influence within the Constellation. In all this, the client can also enter and leave some of the figures several times. This goes on till

Use of Sheets of Paper

we reach a conclusion that brings greater understanding and harmony.

The subjects especially receptive to the Knowing Field, even with eyes closed, can perceive whether, without their knowing it, I move the sheets of paper from their position or change their direction. During the representation I will at times ask the client to close her eyes while I change the configuration of the representation, and I will invite her to sense any changes she might perceive. When a certain configuration gives a particularly positive result, I will ask the client to open her eyes and look at the resulting changes. This way of proceeding is in line with the old Family Constellations in which Hellinger worked mainly on the structural plane, according to the Orders of Love. I use this procedure on some occasions, above all when we reach an impasse or the client is not very receptive to the movements of the Soul. If the client is unreceptive to the Knowing Field, I will let her keep her eyes open, reposition the sheets and ask her how the new arrangement looks to her. These various technical adaptations necessarily consider the client's typology: visual, auditory, kinesthetic. However, I generally prefer to let myself be guided by the movements of the Soul, because one way or another they always lead to the most harmonious solution.

During the representation the client may feel herself pulled in a certain direction, sometimes with her look, sometimes her whole body. If in that area there are no other figures, I will add a sheet of paper and ask her who is in that place. Other times the client may feel her legs give way, so I will invite her to follow her body till, usually, she will sit on her knees or lie supine on the floor. I will then ask the client who is the deceased person next to her, and I will place a sheet of paper there for that person. All these movements widen the scene and introduce other members of the system who have not yet been taken into consideration or who have been excluded.

In this process the client explores and manifests deep emotions, may mend some significant inner and relational rips, while the Constellation is structurally modified and its configuration changed in the direction of greater harmony and integration.

Giovanna and her son's headaches

Giovanna, a 40-year-old woman, comes to me because of a physical problem from which her 10-year-old son Andrea is suffering: chronic painful headaches that have no precise medical explanation. At the first session, she tells me about this disturbance that has worried her and her husband for some years, and about the many medical treatments that have never resolved the problem. The woman has called me

Use of Sheets of Paper

because a friend told her the Family Constellations could resolve the situation.

I explain to her that the Family Constellations are a psychological technique that can, however, help reveal whether a physical disturbance has a systemic-relational origin, but it can in no way replace medical care. I say that I cannot guarantee a result.

The woman tells me about her desperation and how she and her husband have already "tried everything". Given that her friend solved a serious problem with the Family Constellations, she wanted to try it even if it were to produce nothing concrete. So I decide to continue the session by exploring the emotions linked to the problem.

At the end of the meeting I suggest to her a workshop in group Family Constellations, but for organizational reasons it is not possible. We make another appointment for an Individual Constellation.

At the second meeting I explain to Giovanna how an Individual Constellation is done and we decide to place in scene the current family: Giovanna, her husband and the child. We take three sheets of paper, write their names on them, and the woman takes a place on the floor. Andrea is at the center, mother on the left, father on the right. At first glance it all seems right, a good arrangement. The family is united and each is in place.

PRACTICE

I introduce the woman into the representation and place her in her role. She is worried about her son and moves closer to him. So I put the sheet representing the mother a bit closer to the son. I then put her in her husband's role. He too is worried about his son and moves closer to Andrea. I move the father's sheet closer to the son's too. This arrangement shows me that the parents are this close to their son for an important reason. This configuration usually happens when someone's life is at risk. I make no comment and place Giovanna in the son's place.

In representing her son, Giovanna feels weak, her legs start to give way and she can't stay standing up. I tell her to follow her body and she lies down. She tells me she is tired and feels better lying down. So I tell her it is not a question of tiredness, she is representing Andrea and feeling what he feels. Andrea, putting himself on the ground like that, is going towards someone dead. "Who is there by your side?". Suddenly Giovanna gets upset because she remembers an abortion... many years have passed and she hadn't thought about it. It was a painful experience she had before Andrea was born. So I add a sheet for this unborn baby and continue speaking with Andrea. During a representation, in speaking to the client I use the name of the person she is representing, to enhance direct communication and help her identify with what she is doing. I ask Andrea how he is feeling, whether he thinks it is to do with a sibling, and what he feels toward him or her. He says it is a boy and that next to him he feels good: it is the only place where he feels at peace.

After having explored what Andrea experiences, I place his sheet in the new position, and Giovanna in the role of the aborted child, next to Andrea. "How do you feel?". Giovanna has trouble identifying with him. I ask her to breathe deeply with her mouth open and at the end of each exhalation to say: "Mom". This technique is very useful for resolving an "interrupted movement". She starts to breathe like this and after a while says: "I have a headache and am angry!". "With whom are you angry?", I ask. "With Mom!". I tell her to keep breathing and invite her to yell and punch and stomp with all her might. Her voice and anger grow more intense till she starts crying her eyes out. All the desperation of this rejected child comes out in this way. I put my hand on her heart, she continues to cry, and slowly she begins to relax. In the Family Constellations I work with the body to bring out and transform deep primary emotions. In my experience I have noticed that the result is effective to the extent that we get a deep and thorough integration of all that has been removed.

After this first phase I ask the baby his name. I usually prefer the children themselves to give themselves a name. He says he is called Enrico. "Enrico, look at your mother and tell her: "I exist! I want to live!" Enrico repeats this with intensity and emotion. So I ask the woman to put herself in

PRACTICE

her role and write on the unborn baby's sheet his name: Enrico.

The woman looks at the baby and kneels beside him. I move Andrea's sheet and put it next to that of his father. I leave Giovanna next to her child. It is a moment of deep love and tenderness. She welcomes him and looks at him with love. She cries. I perceive that she feels responsible for what has happened. I ask her how it came about and she tells me they were young, not yet married, and had big economic difficulties, but that if she could go back she would not make the same choice. I tell her to look at her child and say: "I take responsibility for what happened. Enrico, you are my little one!". Giovanna sees herself in this affirmation and is very moved in repeating it. And she imagines holding and lulling her little one, and does it with love. I give her all the time she needs for this poignant experience. Afterwards I ask her to place herself in the father's role, and have him, in turn, encounter Enrico. I ask him too to say the same sentence. And so I continue to facilitate this encounter between the parents and this baby, until little Enrico feels well, acknowledged, and all right.

I put all in a new arrangement where Enrico has his place next to his brother Andrea, between the parents. All feel at peace and in harmony. Thus I close the Constellation and reserve, as always, ten minutes before ending the session.

Use of Sheets of Paper

We return to our chairs and Giovanna is rather upset by this experience. She never expected anything of the kind. I listen with empathy, while I visualize next to her the children and her husband. I feel much empathy for Enrico; inwardly I too welcome him. I feel all are now at peace.

Giovanna wants to know if she may talk to her husband and Andrea about what happened in the session. I suggest she wait three weeks, and to keep it to herself as it must be assimilated. Assagioli, founder of Psychosynthesis, has this to say on the subject: "It is not what you eat that nourishes you: it is what you digest".

At the end of the three weeks, she may speak with her husband about it, and the only action I suggest she take is to add a seat at their dining table. One day, when they feel they can, they will be able to tell Andrea about Enrico.

I see Giovanna again a month later. She tells me of some very touching dreams she has had. She dreamed several times of hugging and cuddling a baby. This month she had a menstrual cycle that was much heavier than usual. And she tells me how after three weeks she shared this experience with her husband. Meanwhile Andrea has not had any headaches. It seems all is going well. Giovanna, however things may turn out, feels the Constellation has been a positive experience and has brought her closer to her husband.

PRACTICE

A year later I meet Giovanna at a group Constellations workshop. She comes happily up to me and says Andrea has never again suffered from headaches. I am surprised and tell her I am very pleased that all is resolved. Every time, I myself am amazed at the efficacy of the Family Constellations.

How do you explain Andrea's headaches considering the Orders of Love? Enrico had been forgotten and his parents had not suffered enough for his loss. Enrico's suffering, too, had not been taken into consideration. Thus Andrea manifested in his body Enrico's suffering. This shows an entanglement with an excluded member of the family. Once Enrico's anger, pain and desperation was recognized, once the parents acknowledged their responsibility and suffered sufficiently for this loss, and once the little one was finally recognized and honored, the whole system was restructured towards greater harmony. When that happens, any kind of disturbance that has a systemic-relational origin has no more reason for persisting and disappears straightaway. In this sense the Family Constellations have something magical about them, not in the esoteric sense, but because of their capacity to reveal the wondrous sacrality of existence.

Free Space

by Marco Moretti

I started using the Individual Constellations in free space when I discovered the technique "by chance" in 2010, and I don't know if other therapists know and use it. A client of mine who had just participated in some group Family Constellations workshops came to me for individual therapy. During the sessions we first used the Individual Constellations with the sheets of papers, but bit by bit I realized that the sheets were becoming a hindrance to in-depth exploration. So one day I decided to do without them and use the space with no demarcations, thus leaving the client free to move while she visualized the representation in the space.

Thanks to this experience and to further developments with other clients, I realize that this is the Individual Constellations technique I prefer. Why I prefer it is that it leaves the field open to any perceptive experience coming from the Knowing Field, especially from the Spiritual Consciousness, thus permitting the same depth that you can reach in the group Family Constellations.

This technique has shown me that space behaves like a kind of three-dimensional screen onto which the Knowing Field projects the information about the family system the client decides to evoke. Perhaps science will one day be able

PRACTICE

to explain this phenomenon. For my part, it is enough to know that it works and is useful in therapeutic work, as I have amply proven.

This technique cannot be used with all clients because it requires excellent receptivity to the Knowing Field, a capacity that is developed through participating in the group Family Constellations, or else through means such as meditation or other activities that develop the intuition.

If a client comes to me and has already actively participated in a few group Family Constellations, I then prefer to use the technique of free space in individual work. I have also used it with people who had never done group workshops but had a good intuitive ability.

How I proceed

To practice the Individual Constellations in free space you need at least 3 x 3 meters, the same as with the sheets of paper. My decision whether to practice this technique or not is based on the premises described in the previous section. I try, however, to assess whether it is easier for the client to use the technique with the sheets of paper, or without.

Just as in the group representations, the free space technique must be uninterrupted from start and finish. This

Free Space

is because the client enters a state of deep absorption that is better left unhindered so the representation can flow freely.

Given that this kind of technique is close to the Spiritual Family Constellations, it is often not necessary to stage the whole family. In the Spiritual Constellations you start with few elements, often just one, and add only the essential, which is manifest through the Knowing Field, and which, through movements of the soul, finds its solution with fluidity. Therefore, when I have agreed with the client on the kind of work to be explored, I often simply point to a spot in the space, in which to represent something, and then place the client in that position. Or else I ask the client where she pictures herself and another significant element, and then get the representation going.

For example, if Giovanna, of the previous subchapter, had been even more receptive to the Knowing Field, I simply would have pointed to a spot in the space and said: "There is the origin of your son's headaches", and I would have placed her on that spot. What might have happened after this? Since I have used this technique hundreds of times, I can try to imagine the outcome. She probably would have collapsed onto the floor and shown the physical sensations and the emotions of the aborted baby. I would have helped her explore these sensations and emotions, then asked her to look around her and see what else was present in the scene. The Knowing Field does in fact allow a receptive person to "see" the scene and the people who compose it as images projected onto the nearby space. Thus, probably, she would have "seen" the baby brother, would have realized she was an aborted baby, and afterwards would have "seen" his mother and father too.

During this kind of representation the first thing I do is help the client to deepen and explore her sensations and emotions, and afterwards to "see", or imagine, who are the other actors in the scene and where they are placed. When the client has visualized the other figures who compose the representation, and when she is well enough oriented in the scene, I then move her and introduce another representative, the one I regard most significant. In this work not necessarily do you perceive all the characters of the scene straightaway: often you identify them bit by bit. This phenomenon facilitates the therapist, who thus knows in which other figure to place the client. Should more than one figure emerge at the same time, you must let yourself be guided by your own perception of the Knowing Field and by your own experience, to decide in which figure to place the client. As I described in the preceding section, very often I have the client represent all the characters in the scene. As I proceed with this kind of exploration, the perceptions become ever clearer and more information and insights emerge to facilitate the movement of the whole representation towards the resolution.

In this process I help the client go along with the movements of the soul so that all the representation finds its dynamic. When you use free space, it often happens that while the client represents a certain figure she can also "see" the dynamism of the others, just as occurs in the group Family Constellations. In other words, whereas with the sheets of paper the representatives are in a sense "set" in their positions, with free space the other figures are also free to move about in the perceived space visualized by the client. Thus, for example, while the client approaches another person, she would be able to "see" this other either backing away or approaching, an eventuality that does not occur with the sheets of paper.

Virginia the quick-tempered

Virginia, a 30-year-old woman, comes to me because she is having considerable family conflicts. Since enrolling at University she has lived about a hundred kilometers from her original family. Every time she goes to her parents' home conflicts arise.

In the first session she tells me about her arguments with her mother, father and sister. Virginia also tells me she has already had two years of psychotherapy that allowed her to raise her self-esteem but did not help change the family situation.

Virginia's problem is that when in the family she is always very nervous, on the defensive, has fits of rage that burst out in words and actions more than would be expected in relation to what provoked them.

I establish a relationship of trust and empathy with her. It seems to me that already in the first session we work well together, because I sense we are in tune. Virginia is intelligent, with excellent capacity for insight.

At the second session she relates a nightmare that woke her up with a start the night of our previous encounter: she is in a dark place and from a distance seems to see a violent and bloody scene. The scene changes and she sees a woman being raped by a man. Suddenly she wakes up in anguish. I listen, and help her bring these images into focus and to link them with emotions and sensations in the here and now. In this in-depth work emerge many mental associations with what she told me the last time: the angry outbursts and the exasperated conflicts she experiences in the family. At the end of the session she feels a bit more serene and aware.

At the third session Virginia says she has had a very heated conflict with her mother, but that it had produced the effect of a rapprochement. At last they could talk and understand each other. This was new. Strangely, this conflict, instead of making her distancing herself and shut herself off,

Free Space

caused a breakthrough in their relationship. Virginia is very pleased and wishes to establish an understanding relationship with her father and sister too. I speak to her about the Family Constellations and say that next time, if she is interested, we can use this technique to make a further breakthrough in the family situation.

At the fourth encounter we prepare for the Individual Constellation. From the previous sessions I have noticed Virginia's good intuitive ability, so I choose a representation in free space. I briefly describe the technique and point to a spot opposite us where she is to be. Since it is the first time Virginia is working with this technique, I decide she should represent herself for the time being.

I place Virginia in her spot and ask her to visualize her family in the space in front of her. She sees them in a row facing her, and starts to get edgy. Her body stiffens and begins to move nervously here and there. Her attention, like that of a predator, is attracted by her father's back. The representation starts moving, the father moves and she begins to follow him. It is all very strange. The atmosphere seems rather delirious. Virginia grows more and more agitated and suddenly moves to another part of the room. Everything stops. Virginia is now looking in another direction.

I ask Virginia who she's looking at. I ask her this because, as I explained in the last section, every gesture and movement has a relational meaning. In a representation, when someone starts looking in a certain direction, it is because she is looking at someone. Since Virginia had not visualized any of her family in that direction, I ask her who is there before her. Virginia widens her eyes a little and tells me she sees a man. I have her describe him to me, and suddenly she remembers the nightmare she had the month before. Now she feels hate for this man, clenches her fists, feels a tingling in her arms and an irresistible urge to stab him in the shoulders. I perceive in this dynamic the energy of the killer. I realize that in Virginia's family there has been a murder, and that she is entangled with the murderer.

I ask Virginia to enter the figure of this man. She moves, enters it, and starts to feel weak and collapse to the ground. I have her describe her physical sensations and her emotions. She feels a sharp pain in the back; she is distressed. She sees a night scene in the rain, at the beginning of the 1900's, where another man repeatedly stabs him in the back because of a betrayal. He is on the ground in a pool of blood. He knows he is a relative of Virginia on her father's side.

I ask Virginia to enter the figure of the perpetrator, who is standing beside the stabbed man. When he (Virginia, as perpetrator has become a "he") does so, he is furious and starts vigorously raising and lowering his arm, as though he were stabbing the man (victim). After killing him, he stands up and wants to possess the woman for whom he committed this murder. He sees her there next to him, and imagines raping her. I then ask Virginia to enter the figure of this woman. In doing so, she feels the violence of that act, but she also feels possessed by the man, whom she hates and loves at the same time. She feels she is his possession, just as she feels he belongs to her. It is a perverse relationship. As we gradually explore this relationship, the bond loosens more and more.

When Virginia enters the figure of the perpetrator once again, she feels less and less hate, more tiredness, and finally compassion for his victim. She is no longer interested in the woman, and wants to put an end to all that hate. So I ask her to move out of the scene, enter herself, and visualize from outside her dead relative, the murderer, and his woman. I ask if she feels like kneeling. She does so and begins to cry – out of pain and compassion for all that useless violence. I place a hand on her back. She remains kneeling, breathes deeply, and gradually feels more relaxed and at peace. We stay there awhile till she is calm and detached from the scene, as if it no longer belonged to her. I then ask her to enter the role of her father and whether he, too, feels he can kneel. He does so too, and feels at peace. Now everything is right.

Virginia stands up. I ask her to re-enter herself and to visualize her family again. She sees her father, mother and sister beside her. Now she feels differently: she can look at them with love, and wants to hug them. She sees they are looking at her with love too, and expressing their affection. It is an intensely moving moment. I sense in this image tenderness, strength and cohesion at once.

We end the representation. It has been very deep work and Virginia feels the need to stay quiet. She tells me only that she feels well and at peace.

At the fifth session Virginia comes with a new look. She is more beautiful, has taken trouble over her appearance. I pay her a compliment and ask her how she feels. She says that since last time she has felt serene, in harmony, and noticed balance between the left and right side of her body. Yet it is as if she had lost part of herself, as if something that before was part of her had disappeared. We talk about this and Virginia realizes that what has disappeared is her entanglement with the perpetrator. A few days before she spoke with her family on the phone and was not nervous, but calm. She feels something important has changed. Now she wants to look after herself and get along with her family.

At the sixth encounter Virginia tells me she has seen her family again and things have inexplicably changed. She hasn't had any more conflicts with them and they have been able to understand one another, as had already happened between her and her mother. She has spoken with her father about the Constellation and he seemed curious about it, also because for years he had suffered from inexplicable back pain. The breakthrough has occurred. Virginia can't explain how this is possible, but is very happy about the result.

The past may be left behind only if we process the grief over the dead, the victims; and if we let the perpetrators process their grief over the victims. It's the only way. Thus we can kneel before them and look to the future. Thus the dead too find peace: only in this way. And the living are free to go and meet their future. Grief therefore is a condition for putting an occurrence to rest and allowing reconciliation – shared grief (Hellinger, 2006).

[...] If we adopt the distinction between good and evil, we can no longer be of help. As soon as we make that decision, we exclude someone. We will take a stance against someone we perceive as bad. We can only truly help if everyone obtains a place in our heart, if we acknowledge that everyone has the same right to exist and that everyone is in some way entangled, even if we would want to call him bad. We too can be entangled in the good and believe ourselves to be right. [...] Great help, and help as an art, need strength. And they need perspective. And they need this love that accepts everything (Hellinger, 2006).

Visualization

by Marco Moretti

I learned to use visualization for couples and family psychotherapy in 2005 with Sheldon Kramer, a psychotherapist from San Diego with a psychosynthetic and systemic-relational approach.

Kramer accompanied us in the exploration of various psycho-bodily, imaginative and meditative techniques that we could use in clinical sessions. His psycho-bodily-relational-spiritual work (Kramer, 1995) is directed at the inner and outer family and aimed at the healing of intra-psychic, intra-familial and intergenerational wounds. It is an integrated approach that masterfully joins the experiences of Roberto Assagioli (1965; 2007), Virginia Satir (1967; 1988) and James Framo (1992).

In the years following, I used these techniques, combining them with my experience of the Family Constellations, and applying to them the principles and systemic laws formulated by Bert Hellinger.

The Individual Constellations that I have described in the preceding section are realized and moved in physical space: with visualization you proceed in the same way but inside mental space. These techniques, therefore, can be used by clients who have an excellent imaginative ability. They are undoubtedly the hardest to practice, yet when that is possible they achieve deep results.

Visualization has a profoundly restructuring power because it acts directly on the mental images, thus shaping the unconscious. Not uncommonly, when this technique is used, the client enters a state of hypnotic trance, that is, in a state of deep inner absorption. This makes the therapist more responsible, because with visualization he penetrates the client's deepest psychic meanderings. For this reason, of the techniques described, the ones that use visualization are the riskiest, and can be suggested only to clients who are emotionally stable and who have normal psychic functioning.

I use visualization in systemic work with three different techniques: Healing the Inner Family, Inner Constellation, and Ascent and Dialogue with the Self.

Healing the Inner Family is one of the techniques used by Kramer (1995); its aim is to have the person meet the inner family and heal its wounds. The Inner Constellation is specifically a Family Constellation that takes place inwardly and is my adaptation of this technique combined with the use of visualization. The Ascent and Dialogue with the Self is my systemic modification of a visualization suggested by Assagioli (Moretti, 2010) and aims at putting the family in touch with the family's Soul, or as Hellinger (2008) calls it, the Great Soul.

Visualization

The choice of technique depends on the client's characteristics and needs, the problem presented, and the goals of the therapeutic project.

Healing the Inner Family works for the care of "object relations". The premise is that our inner world has been formed because of experiences with the external world made of relationships that the family of origin has maintained with us. According to this theory, children internalize actual characteristics of the parents, or caregivers, and their conjugal relationship, and all of this is incorporated in their personality, determining their behavior and future affective choices (Framo, 1992). In addition, people relate to their internal parts (subpersonalities) in much the same way their parents, or caregivers, related to those same parts of them (Schwartz, 1995). From the viewpoint of the principles and systemic laws conceived by Hellinger, the individual's biophysical constitution is not due only to the original family's influence, but also to that of the preceding generations, even when the individual has never been in contact with them. So Kramer's original technique, has been adapted to make the systemic vision even vaster and more inclusive, with the goal of healing the suffering in family relations of the past, the wounds of the inner world.

The Inner Constellation works both on the family of origin, as it is in the present moment, and on the actual one or on any other kind of relationship, problem or pathology, just as do all the other techniques of Family Constellations. This technique is directed at the relationships as they are.

The Ascent and Dialogue with the Self is useful for all those who are interested in contacting the spiritual dimension for receiving higher guidance. It consists in a symbolic ascent towards the peak of a mountain together with all the members of the family, original or actual, to meet the Soul of the family in the form of an Old Sage or a spiritual being.

These techniques demand much mental energy and should therefore be proposed only if the client has slept and eaten enough, and has not taken drugs and drank alcohol in the previous twelve hours.

How I proceed

These three techniques require the client to be sitting comfortably, with the trunk upright: not lying down, to ensure she does not fall asleep. A comfortable armchair or divan are both fine, and it is best if the client's head is supported so the neck muscles can relax.

In applying these techniques, the therapist dialogues with the client's unconscious. Note that the unconscious takes language literally.

Visualization

I introduce each technique with a short relaxation, in a calm and deep tone of voice: "Close your eyes and take a deep breath... Relax... Feel the contact of your feet with the floor... the contact of your thighs with the armchair... the contact of your back with the armchair... Relax the muscles of your neck and let your head subside backward... Take another deep breath and relax all the muscles of your body...", and so on, for not more than five minutes. I then proceed with the visualization.

Healing the Inner Family

This technique is composed of five stages in which you visualize and work with the original family as it has been internalized in childhood:

1. Orientation
2. Recognition
3. Acceptance
4. Coordination
5. Inner coherence

1. **Orientation**. The first stage is the visualization of the childhood home (if there are more than one, the first image that comes up) and inside it all the members of the family

who live there, including the client as a child. You guide her as an external observer in orienting herself and moving about in the house to observe and describe all the members of the family, including herself. The aim is for her to become aware of the situation and observe the different expressions, emotions and attitudes of all family members as well as the relationship between them. The visualization is conducted slowly, with pauses, thus giving the client time to perceive the images adequately. Short, clear phrases are used:

"Visualize your home at the time you were little... Inside is your family... Look and see where they are... Are they all together or in different rooms? Go up to them all and look closely at their expressions... What are their emotions?... Their attitudes?... What relationship is there between them?...". In this stage the client is orienting herself in the home and looking carefully at all members of the family. This work amplifies the memory and allows the client to remember details she had forgotten. In this stage it is useful to have her look at the home, whether there are objects, clothes, photos, or anything else that might belong to some deceased, forgotten or excluded member. It is important also to notice where the family members are looking, because the direction of their gaze always indicates the presence of another person, dead or alive. And if someone is supine, it probably means this person is lying next to a deceased one. All these details are useful for placing in scene possibly

Visualization

missing people, with whom other members of the family might be entangled, to allow the system to attain harmony.

2. **Recognition**. In the second stage you help the client recognize who are the most suffering people and what the suffering is. "Who is the most suffering person?... From what expression and attitude do you understand this suffering?... What is it about?... How do you feel about him or her?... Are there other suffering people?...". And so on, up until she recognizes each person's suffering.

3. **Acceptance**. In this stage you help the client accept the suffering or the conflicts. This happens through the client's deep contact with her sensations, emotions and needs. You have the client identify with the most suffering person, and one by one with all the others.

"Now identify with the person who is suffering the most, enter into him or her... What sensations and emotions do you experience?... Where do you feel them in your body?... In this phase sensations and emotions are explored in depth. You try to widen everything that is encountered. When the client identifies a part of the body in which she feels the emotions, you ask her to put a hand on that part and get deeply in touch with it. For example: "I feel despair". "In which part of your body do you feel it?". "In the chest". "Place a hand on your chest and breathe into that spot"... "Get in touch with your despair"... After thoroughly exploring the sensations and emotions the need is identified: "What do you need?...".

4. **Coordination**. In the fourth stage you make the suffering people relate to the rest of the family through deep communication, thus encouraging a new inner organization. Each contact with the parties follows the order: recognition, acceptance and communication (through deep listening, empathy, understanding, negotiation and collaboration).

"To whom do you wish to communicate this need of yours?..." In this way the client finds herself singling out another member of the family and deciding whether to communicate to him her need. If she decides she does not want to, you may ask her: "Who should know this need of yours?" At that point you may ask the client if she is prepared to communicate her need. If not, you could ask her to tell the person who should know her need: "I'm not ready to let you know that I need...". In this way her unwillingness to communicate is respected, even as she communicates it. If the client stiffens, it is best to interrupt the visualization. If she is interested in continuing, you can proceed. It may be that the family members are distributed in other rooms. In this case the therapist asks the person who wishes to communicate to someone his or her need to move towards that person. If the client is ready to communicate her need, you ask her to start from the center of the heart: "Go towards (the person to whom she wants to communicate the need)...

Visualization

Look at him/her... From the center of your heart say: I need to...". In this phase the suffering due to an interrupted movement towards the loved one may arise. In this case you must help the client disinhibit the movement and bring it to conclusion, as described in the preceding sections.

When the client has communicated her need to another family member, you ask her how she feels. You then have her exit that figure and help her identify with this other. "Now come out of ... and enter into ... Look at (the suffering person)... What do you feel when (the suffering person) tells you he needs ...?... Where do you feel it in your body?... Place a hand there and breathe into that spot...". You proceed like this, exploring the sensations and emotions of this person. You then have this person communicate again with the previous figure. For example thus: "When you told me you needed love, I was moved, I feel it in my heart". "Now put your hand on your heart, look at (the suffering person) and say: your words move me". In this way you encourage a deep dialogue between the various people involved.

If the client has singled out more than one suffering person, you go back to stage 3 and proceed to help her identify with these other figures, till stages 3 and 4 are completed.

5. **Inner coherence**. This phase represents the result in which the family finds harmonious cohesion.

PRACTICE

The first stage of this visualization can also be used by itself as an assessment, to evaluate the client's situation and the kind of work to be explored afterwards.

Healing the Inner Family is very deep work that usually requires a few sessions. To pace it properly, you should interrupt it appropriately: that is, in a satisfactory way, the moment the client has completed one stage, or one of the intermediate phases, that is, at the moment she has greater strength and feels well. You should never interrupt it at a painful or anguishing moment. Nor should you keep going at all costs if the client is tired.

When you have decided to end the visualization, you should have the client leave the character she was representing and make her take the position of an external observer. You then ask her to distance herself from the scene, look at it to see what has changed and what she experiences in observing it. Finally you ask her to take a few deep breaths and let that image go. The client can then, in her own time, open her eyes and resume contact with her body and everything around it.

You may end the session by asking the client to reflect on the experience: "What do you think we have worked on today?... What does it mean to you?...". The therapist can give signs of acknowledging the client's experience, thus encouraging her awareness. Finally, he may encourage the activation of her will by helping her to state her aims: "How

Visualization

could you take into your daily life what you have learned or the qualities you have evoked today?...".

In the next sessions you will note any changes in the qualities of the images, and in the characteristics and arrangement of the family. And proceeding gradually in this work, takes one towards the final stage of coherence in the inner family.

Inner Constellation

The working of inner and outer systems is similar, and what is interesting is that they are mutually interdependent: when one changes, so can does the other.

The client's internal and external worlds comprise one large system, operating according to the same principles and responsive to the same techniques. In addition, because systems that interface come to reflect one another, changes at one level can produce parallel changes at other level. (Schwartz, 1995).

Thus when we work with an Inner Constellation – the intrapersonal relationships – we are also influencing the interpersonal relationships.

Leading an Inner Constellation requires familiarity both the visualization techniques and with the conducting of

PRACTICE

Family Constellations. Whereas the technique of Healing the Inner Family tends to be structured, the Inner Constellation is considerably unpredictable compared to a Constellation in free space. In fact during a visualization the unconscious can present odd images that the therapist must be able to manage. They may for example be unusual scenes or episodes that seem to have nothing to do with the client's current life. Everything that emerges during this kind of work needs to be integrated. The therapist should therefore know how to deal usefully and constructively with any image that arises. For these reasons it is best to start from a well-defined image, for instance, by staging the original or current family, or a precise relationship.

The Inner Constellation consists of three stages:

1. Observation
2. Coordination
3. Conclusion

After the preliminary phase of relaxation, you ask the client to imagine a big, empty room in which to represent the various characters, including herself. For example, in the case of the original family: "Imagine a big, empty room... In it are the members of your original family, including you... Describe what you see...". In this first stage the client is a

Visualization

point of observation that can move and describe the representation in all its details.

You then invite the client to look better at some important details: "Now observe and describe their physical position... their expression... the direction of their gaze...". The client describes the members of her family and the relationship between them. An interesting aspect is how the client sees herself from the outside, how she describes herself and sees herself in relation to the others.

The details highlighted in this stage can help the therapist understand the family dynamics. Furthermore, they help him see if there are other figures the client has not yet visualized. If a family member looks down to the ground, you can ask: "Observe who is there on the ground where he/she is looking...". This is a request that directs the client's attention to a yet undisclosed element of the scene. The same applies if a living member is lying on the ground: "Observe who is on the ground next to him/her...". Or again, if one member is looking elsewhere compared to all the others: "See in whose direction he/she is looking...". It has been found, in fact, that in the Family Constellations the representatives are always turning their gaze towards someone, never something. The same holds for bodily movements, which are always movements of approach or distancing relative to someone, never something. In this first stage, therefore, other figures could be disclosed, and you should help the client see how the arrangement of the representation changes.

Whether other figures reveal themselves or not, it is possible that the members of the family change position and the representation modifies its configuration dynamically. The therapist may ask: "See if the family members move or if they stay still... What do you see?...". When the scene has stabilized, you may ask the client: "What do you experience in seeing this scene?...". This is a directional question that tends to involve the client emotionally. It gives the therapist the chance to explore her emotions. When the client is emotionally involved, she may be introduced into the representation. Thus you pass to the next stage.

The stage of coordination consists in the therapist helping the client identify with all the family members, one by one, and each time placing her in relation to the others, to explore the whole representation. At the start it is best to ask the client to enter into herself: "Now enter into the representation and identify with yourself... Look at the representation from this viewpoint... What do you see?... What do you feel?...". From this point of view the client's perception might change. You then proceed to explore sensations and emotions. "This emotion you are feeling: in which part of your body do you feel it?...". You work to amplify and broaden whatever emerges, and put it all in relation to some other member of the family. "What does it

Visualization

make you feel (desperate, angry, and so on)?... What do you need?... To whom do you want to say it?...". And so you proceed, placing the client in communication with the other members of the family. While the client speaks with another member, she may also see the other's emotional reaction. "How does this person react to your words?... And how does this make you feel?...". All that emerges can be further explored. You then ask the client to identify with another member with whom she has opened communication, and as before, to explore the sensations and emotions. You carry on like this, encouraging deep communication between all the members. This work continues till the representation finds its solution and is configured in a more harmonious way.

The Inner Constellation usually takes less time than Healing the Inner Family. Nevertheless, it too may be interrupted and resumed at a later session. You may interrupt at the end of the first stage, or at another moment when the client has strength and feels well. At the end of the visualization it is useful to make her assume the position of external observer and look at the scene to see what has changed and what she feels in looking at it. After this, the client may open her eyes again and, in her own time, resume contact with her body and everything around her.

PRACTICE

Ascent and Dialogue with the Self

This visualization is useful, at a later session, for concluding the work of Healing the Inner Family or of an Inner Constellation. The two preceding techniques work on a horizontal plane (relationship between the parts): this last works on a vertical plane (relationship with the transpersonal Self). It is thus useful for integrating previous work, consolidating the family coherence, or helping the client find answers to questions that only the Great Soul is required to give.

If the client has never worked with the Family Constellations it would be better to avoid this visualization, because contact with the transpersonal Self, the Great Soul, usually amplifies all that has been removed or repressed, especially the shadow. The energy of the transpersonal Self, in fact brings with it an energetic voltage that acts to intensify everything that has been concealed or excluded, with the aim of bringing it to light and reintegrating it (Moretti, 2004). Thus, if the client has not done work in Family Constellations, after this visualization she might see a worsening of certain problems or disorders in the family, which are caused by grief, events not yet processed, other unacceptable events, and entanglements with excluded family members.

Visualization

The Ascent and the Dialogue with the Self consists in four stages:

1. Ascent
2. Request and listening
3. Recording
4. Evaluation

1. **Ascent**. "Imagine you are at the foot of a mountain with all members of your family, no one excluded... Look at each one of them... Then look nearby: you see a path leading to the summit... Up there lives an Old Sage, a Master or a spiritual being who will welcome you and answer all your questions... Feel your aspiration to meet him/her. Imagine walking with your whole family along this path... While climbing, help and encourage one another... and feel the air growing fresher and lighter... Observe the view and the horizon widening as you continue to climb together higher and higher... Feel an ever-greater sense of elevation as you near the peak... At the top is a clearing... Wait for everyone to arrive... In this clearing a spiritual being is waiting for you... Observe and approach him/her...".

2. **Request and listening**. "Formulate in turn a precise question: to give you directions about your family situation or to answer a question of yours... Each one of you, after asking it, listens to the Master's answer... At the end you may

PRACTICE

ask three more questions… Give all the other members the freedom to communicate with the Master… Listen to what they say to each other… Finally, thank the Master and say goodbye…".

3. **Recording**. "In your own time, open your eyes and resume contact with your body and surroundings… Now you can write down your visualization, impressions, emotions, the messages you have all received, and what you have learned from this experience…".

4. **Evaluation**. You help the client reflect on this experience and assess the directions contained in it, relative to their usefulness at this moment in her life and family relationships. To end, it may be useful to activate the will by asking the client: "How could you take into your daily life what you have learned today or the qualities you have evoked?…".

This kind of visualization may also be done in the couple or with other family members. In that case, at the end of the third stage they share the experience with one another, compare and integrate the information received, and finally, evaluate all together how to apply it concretely in daily life.

Visualization

Brigitta and the family inheritance

Brigitta is a middle-aged woman who has just done an individual journey in Psychosynthesis and Family Constellations with me. It has helped her "loosen some knots" that were stopping her from expressing the freedom of her soul. Two months ago she lost her father. She has now come back to resolve the question of inheritance.

Her mother left to her three children a lovely house in the historic center of town, as well as a debt of several thousand euros. Brigitta and her younger sister have not been able to pay this debt and would like to sell their mother's house to divide the money and solve the economic matters. The eldest sister, however, doesn't want to know about selling the mother's house... The result is that the sisters are entering conflict with one another.

Brigitta describes the situation to me: her sense of impotence, her worry, and her inability to communicate with her older sister. On the other hand, she has always had an excellent relationship with her younger sister. From when they were little, the mother's pet was the eldest sister, whereas Brigitta and her younger sister were closer to their dad. Their father had the role of mediator in the family, but he, too, died some years ago.

I suggest to Brigitta an Inner Constellation. Brigitta accepts, but she tells me she is worn out and doesn't want to feel poorly, so we agree to do targeted, soft work. I accompany her in a short relaxation, and ask her to visualize the current situation represented by the three sisters and the house, and to picture the three of them and the house in a large space. Brigitta sees the house at the center of the space, herself and her younger sister next to each other near the house, and the older sister on the other side. I ask her to observe all of them. She describes the house as beautiful and strong. She and the younger sister are supporting each other fondly and looking impotently at the big sister, who instead is looking sadly at the house.

I ask Brigitta to identify with the home. The house feels strong, but if it looks at the three sisters it grows weak. Their misunderstandings drain its strength and it feels limited in its freedom, its chance of living its destiny. Next I ask the house to describe the relationship it feels with each of them. The house perceives Brigitta and the younger sister detached from it, whereas it feels a limiting bond with the oldest sister. It sees cord connecting them, and feels it is this cord that is limiting it, but that it is not up to it to release it. I then tell the house to turn to the eldest sister and say: "This bond is limiting me, I need to be free". The sister grows even sadder. The house perceives that this daughter is relating to it as if it were her mother. So I ask it to tell her: "I am not your mother". The daughter starts to cry desperately. The hard

Visualization

person she has always shown herself to be now cries like an abandoned child.

I ask Brigitta to dis-identify from the house and return to looking at the scene as external observer. I then ask her to visualize her mother next to her older sister. The mother looks with love at the daughter, who keeps crying without looking at her. The mother approaches her and says: "I am your mother, this house is not". The daughter looks at the mother and, crying, tells her she misses her terribly. In that moment Brigitta sees the cord that was linking the sister to the house transfer to join the sister and the mother. The house is free and at last the older sister expresses her pain at the loss of her mother, although she had not shed a tear at the funeral. Brigitta takes a deep breath... Then the older sister looks at the younger two and says: "I am suffering because I miss our mother". They smile with love and reply: "We are here with you".

I ask Brigitta to identify with herself. She enters herself. She is at peace, feels harmony and understanding. She breathes deeply. Now she understands her older sister's suffering and realizes she can do nothing but ensure her presence for her. They now look at each other with love and understanding.

We end the Constellation thus, and Brigitta opens her eyes. She didn't imagine that her sister identified the house with their mother. Now she sees why she was closed to their request to sell it. She felt moved seeing her sister cry like a baby. She feels tenderness towards her and understands that they need time to process their grief. The loss of their mother, instead of distancing them, can bring them closer... The three of them are all that is left of the original family.

A few months later Brigitta calls me and tells me that she and her sisters have met in their mother's home to put in order the mother's possessions and clothes. They reminisced about their life with their mother and father, and it was a touching experience that brought them very close to one another. They have reached an agreement and have serenely decided to sell the house.

My experience of leading countless Family Constellations in the last years convinces me more and more that this method – to paraphrase Virginia Satir (1988) – is of great help in learning to replace judgment with exploration, being right with being authentic, anxiety with excitement, and limitations with possibilities.

Conclusions

The Family Constellations are the result of a long journey – combining many therapeutic experiences and involving a constant spiritual evolution – which mirrors not only the professional and personal path of Bert Hellinger, but also the current need to use simple, effective, and at the same time deep, therapeutic methods. We are grateful to Bert Hellinger for having shared with us his knowledge and shown us this new therapeutic horizon.

This manual too stems from the combination of our different approaches, and thus contributes to understanding human beings and their vital relations in their systemic wholeness: physical, psychological, relational and spiritual. We deem this integration indispensable for the healing of humanity.

This work has been possible thanks to our everyday clinical experience and the openness of the clients who have come to us. We are grateful to all who trusted in us and gave us permission to use these techniques, thus enabling us to verify their efficacy, confirmed by the clients' satisfaction and wellbeing.

We are grateful to Jutta ten Herkel, who first read our text and supported us in proceeding with confidence and purpose.

We are grateful to Vivien Reid Ferrucci for having translated this book, and for her helpfulness and kindness.

The experiences we have wished to share are also the fruit of the studies and research that preceded us, just as this knowledge will lead others after us to do further in-depth research. We are grateful to all our teachers for having shared their knowledge with us.

The proverb: "He who knows not the land from which he comes, will not find the land he seeks", expresses well our attitude to the quest, which, from knowledge of and respect for the past, builds a possible and desirable future. The life force consists precisely in continuing to develop and to reach new frontiers.

Marco Moretti and Daniela Poggioli

References

ASSAGIOLI, R. (1922), Martha and Mary, A Study of Outer and Inner Action. Sundial House, Tunbridge Wells, 1966.

ASSAGIOLI, R. (1965), Psychosynthesis. A Manual of Principles and Techniques. Psychosynthesis Research Foundation, New York.

ASSAGIOLI, R. (1967), Panorama del vivere psicologico. Lezioni sulla Psicosintesi, lez. XII, Istituto di Psicosintesi, Firenze.

ASSAGIOLI, R. (2007), Transpersonal Development, The Dimension Beyond Psychosynthesis. Smiling Wisdom, Findhorn.

ASSAGIOLI, R. (1996), Gruppo di Meditazione per la Nuova Era. Istituto Cintamani, Roma.

BATESON, G. (1979), Mind and Nature. A Necessary Unity (Advances in Systems Theory, Complexity, and the Human Sciences). E.P. Dutton, New York.

BATESON, G. (1991), A Sacred Unity. Further Steps to an Acology of Mind. Cornelia & Michael Bessie, New York.

BERNE, E. (1972), What Do You Say After You Say Hello?. Grove Press Inc., New York.

BERTRANDO P., TOFFANETTI, D. (2000), Storia della terapia familiare. Le persone, le idee. Raffaello Cortina Editore, Milano.

References

BERTRANDO, P. (2002), The presence of the third party. Systemic therapy and transference analysis. Journal of Family Therapy, n. 24, pag. 351–368.

BOHM, D. (1980), Wholeness and the Implicate Order. Routledge, London.

BOADELLA, D., LISS, J. (1986), La Psicoterapia del Corpo. Le nuove frontiere tra corpo e mente. Astrolabio, Roma.

BOSCOLO, L., BERTRANDO, P. (1996), Systemic Therapy with Individuals. Karnac Books, London.

BOSZORMENYI-NAGY, I., SPARK, G. (1973). Invisible Loyalties: Reciprocity in intergenerational family therapy. Harper & Row, New York.

DE SARIO, P., FIUMARA, R. (Eds.) (2015), Biosistemica: la scienza che unisce. FrancoAngeli, Milano.

EDELSTEIN, C. (2007), Counselling Sistemico Pluralista. Dalla Teoria alla Pratica. Edizioni Erickson, Trento.

FRAMO J.L. (1992), Family-of-Origin Therapy. An Integenerational Approach. Brunner-Routledge, New York.

GILL, M.M. (1982), Analysis of Transference. Volume I – Theory and Technique. International Universities Press, New York.

GIOMMI, E.R., CRISTOFORI, S. (Eds.) (2009), Il Benessere nelle Emozioni. Manuale di counseling biosistemico. Edizioni La Meridiana, Molfetta (BA).

HALEY, J. (1959), The family of the schizophrenic: A model system. In The Journal of Nervous and Mental Disease, n. 129, pp. 357-374.

HALEY, J. (1976), Problem-Solving Therapy. Jossey-Bass, San Francisco.

HELLINGER, B. (1998), Ordnungen der Liebe. Ein Kurs-Buch von Bert Hellinger. Bert Hellinger.

HELLINGER, B., TEN HÖVEL, G., (2005), Ein Langer Weg. Kösel-Verlag GmbH & Co., München.

HELLINGER, B. (2006), Ordnungen des Helfens. Carl-Auer-Systeme, Heidelberg.

HELLINGER, B. (2008), Die Liebe des Geistes. Hellinger Pubblications.

HELLINGER, B. (2010a), Ordnungen der Liebe. Überblick, wie die Liebe gelingt. Hellinger Pubblications, Berchtesgaden.

HELLINGER, B. (2010b), Erfolge im Leben/Beruf – Erfolgsgeschichten in Unternehmen und im Beruf – Themenbezogene Unternehmens-Beratung. Hellinger Pubblications, Berchtesgaden.

HELLINGER, B. (2013), Wege in eine andere Weite. Das mediale Familien-Stellen. Hellinger Publications, Berchtesgaden.

HOLY BIBLE, King James Version, 1611 Edition. Hendrickson Publishers, Peabody, 2006.

References

JACOBI, J. (1942), The Psychology of CG Jung. Yale University Press, New Haven.

JUNG, C.G. (1952), Synchronizität als ein Prinzip akausaler Zusammenhänge. erstmals veröffentlicht, In: Jung, C.G., Pauli, W., Naturerklärung und Psyche. Rascher Verlag, Zürich.

JUNG, C.G. (1951), Aion. Beiträge zur Symbolik des Selbst. Walter-Verlag, Olten, 1976.

KRAMER, S.Z. (1995), Trasforming the Inner and Outer Family. Humanistic and Spiritual Approaches to Mind-Body System Therapy. The Haworth Press, New York.

LISS, J., STUPIGGIA, M. (Eds.) (2000), La Terapia Biosistemica. Un approccio originale al trattamento psicocorporeo della sofferenza emotiva. Edizioni FrancoAngeli, Milano.

LUDEWIG, K. PFLIEGER, K., WILKEN, U., JAKOBSKÖTTER, G. (1983), Entwicklung eines Verfahrens zur Darstellung von Familienbeziehungen: Das Familienbrett. In Familiendynamik, n. 8, pp. 235-251.

LUDEWIG, K., WILKEN, U. (2000), Das Familienbrett. Hogrefe, Göttingen.

MAHR, A. (1999), Das Wissende Feld: Familienaufstellung als geistig energetisches heilen, In Geistiges heilen für eine neue zeit. Kösel Verlag, Heidelberg.

MORETTI, M. (2004), Due Maestri Un Solo Cuore. Gli insegnamenti universali di Gesù Cristo e di Siddhartha il Buddha. Marco Moretti, Bologna.

MORETTI, M. (2010), La promessa di ciò che puoi essere. Conosci, possiedi e trasforma te stesso. Edizione Magi, Roma.

NANETTI, F. (2014), Cattive compagnie. Manuale di autodifesa dai violenti, dagli aggressivi, dai manipolatori e dai ladri di energia. Edizioni Pendragon, Bologna.

PLATO (2001), Timaeus. Focus Publishing/R. Pullins Co., Newburyport.

ROSENMAN, M.F. (1988), Serendipity and scientific discovery. Journal of Creative Behaviour, vol. 22 (2), pp. 132-138.

SATIR, V. (1967), Conjoint Family Therapy. A Guide to Theory and Techinique (revised edition). Science and Behavior Books, Palo Alto, 1983.

SATIR, V., BALDWIN, M (1983), Satir Step by Step. Science and Behavior Books, Palo Alto.

SATIR, V. (1988), The New Peoplemaking. Science and Behavior Books, Palo Alto.

SCHNEIDER, J.R., SCHNEIDER, S. (2006), Familien- und Systemaufstellungen in der Einzelarbeit mit Hilfe von Figuren. In DE PHILIPP, W. (Ed.) Systemaufstellungen im Einzelsetting. Carl-Auer-Systeme Verlag, Heidelberg.

References

SCHWARTZ, R.C. (1995), Internal Family Systems Therapy. The Guilford Press, New York.

SELVINI PALAZZOLI, M., BOSCOLO, L., CECCHIN, G., PRATA, G. (1980), Hypothesing-cicularity-neutrality. In Family Process, n. 16, pp. 445-453.

SHELDRAKE, R. (1981), A New Science of Life: The Hypothesis of Formative Causation. Blond and Briggs, London.

STAABS, G.V. (1964), Der Scenotest. Huber, Bern.

TRAMONTI, F., FANALI, A. (2013), Identità e Legami. La Psicoterapia Individuale a Indirizzo Sistemico-Relazionale. Giunti, Firenze.

ULSAMER, B. (1999), Ohne Wurzeln Keine Flügel. Die Systemische therapie von Bert Hellinger. Goldmann Verlag, München.

ULSAMER, B. (2001), Das Handwerk des Familien-Stellens. Eine Einführung in die Praxis der systemischen Hellinger-Therapie. Goldmann Verlag, München.

WEBER, G. (1993) (Ed.), Zweierlei Glück. Die systemische Psychotherapie Bert Hellingers. Carl-Auer-Systeme Verlag, Heidelberg.

WINNICOTT, D.W. (1971), Playing & Reality. Tavistock Publications, London.

ABOUT THE AUTHORS

Marco Moretti, is a psychologist and psychotherapist, trained in Biosystemic Psychotherapy, Emotionally Focused Couples Therapy, Family Constellations and Psychosynthesis. He is a member of the *Istituto di Psicosintesi* and of the *Hellinger Sciencia®*.
In his psychosynthetic training he has had personal therapy and supervision with Piero Ferrucci, and he has developed his knowledge of Systemic Therapy through specific training with Bert Hellinger, Sheldon Kramer, Sue Johnson and Paul Greenman.
Currently Moretti collaborates with the *Istituto di Psicosintesi*, the *Accademia di Formazione Umana "Aghape"* and he is a lecturer at the *Istituto di Psicoterapia Sistemica Integrata* (IDIPSI) of Parma on the use of Family Constellations in Individual Therapy. Moretti regularly works with groups and individuals.
Marco Moretti has published two books: *Due maestri un solo cuore* (2004) and *La promessa di ciò che puoi essere* (2010).
E-mail: biopsicosintesi@gmail.com

Daniela Poggioli. Since 1986 she has lived in Bologna and worked there as a psychologist and psychotherapist.
In 1996 she graduated from the School of Specialization in Systemic-Relational Psychotherapy at the *Centro Milanese di Terapia della Famiglia* (Milan Approach©).
Since 2000 she has taken seminars and training in Family Constellations with Bert Hellinger and colleagues.
She is a lecturer at the *Scuola di Specializzazione in Psicoterapia Biosistemica* of Bologna, and at the *Centro Natura* in the training for Natural Wellness Operator. She is a tutor at the *Istituto Italiano di Programmazione Neuro-Linguistica Meta* of Bologna in training on Family Constellations. She works at a private studio and as school counselor at a private school.
E-mail: danielapoggioli56@gmail.com

Made in the USA
Middletown, DE
06 August 2023